CH00669724

THE COMPLETE I
OF JAMES AUSTEN

Autograph MS of part of James Austen's verse in memory of his sister.

Reproduced by kind permission of the Warden and Scholars of Winchester College.

The Complete Poems of James Austen

Jane Austen's eldest brother

*Edited
with Introduction and Notes
DAVID SELWYN*

THE JANE AUSTEN SOCIETY

First published in Great Britain in 2003
by the Jane Austen Society
c/o Jane Austen's House, Chawton, Hampshire

Copyright © 2003 David Selwyn
Introduction and Notes

ISBN 9538174 4 X

In memory of
Joan Austen-Leigh
great-great-grand-daughter of the poet

British Library Cataloguing-in-Publication data
A catalogue record for this book is available from
the British Library

Printed by Sarsen Press, 22 Hyde Street, Winchester SO23 7DR

CONTENTS

Preface	page	vii
Introduction		ix
An Epistle to Fulwar Craven Fowle Esq.ʳ		1
An Elegy – written at Kintbury, Berks		3
The Hermit		5
Prologue to the Tragedy of Matilda		8
Epilogue to the Tragedy of Matilda		9
Prologue to the Rivals		10
Epilogue to the Rivals		11
The Rash Resolution		11
Sonnet to Lady Catherine Powlet		14
Sonnet to Winter		14
Sonnet to Spring		15
Sonnet to Autumn		15
Sonnet to Summer		16
Sonnet on leaving Oxford		16
Lines Addressed to Miss Charlotte Brydges		17
Sonnet to the same		17
Prologue to The Wonder		18
Epilogue to the Comedy of The Wonder		20
Prologue to The Chances		21
Prologue to the Tragedy of Tom Thumb		23
Prologue to a private Theatrical Exhibition		26
Epilogue to the Sultan		27
The Maid of the Moor		29
April 1805 To Mary		33
To Edward On the death of his first Pony		35
To Caroline – On her Birthday		37
To Miss Jane Austen the reputed Author of Sense and Sensibility		39
To Mary, on her Wedding Day		39
Lines written at Kintbury		41
Home		44
Selbourne Hanger		46
Tyger's letter to Caroline		51

Address to Tyger 52
To Edward On planting a lime tree 53
Ulysses announces to Hecuba that the Manes of
    Achilles demand the sacrifice of Polyxena 56
Morning – to Edward 60
Evening – to Edward 65
On refusing a special invitation 67
Lines written at Steventon 70
Autumn 77
The Autumn Walk – To Mary 83
Venta! within thy sacred fane 86
Lines written in the Autumn of 1817 88
The Œconomy of Rural Life 99
Psalms 117
Œnigmas 120
Charades 125

Bibliography 127
Textual Notes 129
Explanatory Notes 147
Index of first lines 190

PREFACE

Only a very small proportion of the poetry written by Jane Austen's eldest brother, James, has ever appeared in print. None was published in his lifetime, nor subsequently by his children, although they preserved it in carefully made copies; and the few samples that have appeared in print in recent times have been quoted largely for biographical purposes. In the selection of Austen family verse made for the Jane Austen Society and published by the Carcanet Press there was space to include only seven of his shorter poems, whereas altogether he wrote more than fifty, some of them of considerable length.

With increasing attention being paid to the literary influences that helped to shape Jane's own writing, however, particularly in respect to the theatre, on which much work has been done, any information about what she read, or saw performed, or perhaps even took part in, is invaluable. Critics have examined the prologues and epilogues that the young James wrote to accompany the plays acted at Steventon rectory during her childhood, and in doing so have aroused considerable interest in the poems themselves; a study such as Constance Walker's paper at the JASNA Conference in 2001 underlined the intrinsic delights of these pieces, quite apart from their usefulness to Jane Austen biographers. But these represent only one facet of James's poetic personality: he continued to write poetry for the rest of his life and much of it is very pleasing. His tribute to his sister on her death has of course long been known. But he never lost his gift for humorous verse, and several of the poems that he wrote for his children gave him an opportunity to indulge it; furthermore he had an artist's eye for natural scenery, which he described in language of gentle and sensitive appreciation, particularly when writing about the local Hampshire country that was so dear to him. The extracts from some of these pieces that have been used as illustrations of various incidents in his life, or in that of other members of the family, have served to whet the appetite for a fuller experience of his poetry, which is here made available, complete, for the first time.

With the exception of the poem in memory of Jane Austen (*Venta! within thy sacred fane*), no autograph text of any verses by James is known to be extant. There are various letters in his hand, as well as the account of a journey to the New Forest and Salisbury made in the summer of 1818; but if any other of his poems has survived, it has not come to light. The earliest copy is of an unattributed poem, *The Maid of the Moor*, in an unknown hand, on paper with a watermark of 1802. Folded in with this are other poems, obviously neat copies, again in an unidentified hand, on sheets with a watermark of 1813. Some of these are incomplete, but I have nevertheless given them as the text, since they were copied in James's lifetime. By far the greatest proportion of the poetry, however, including complete texts of the above poems (with the exception of *The Maid of the Moor*, which exists only in the MS described above), is in three MS albums made up in the early 1830s. One is in the hand of Anna Lefroy, one probably in that of Caroline Austen and the third was possibly copied by James Edward Austen-Leigh, though the hand is not immediately recognizable: logic would suggest, however, that each of James's children wished to have a copy. Full details of these and other MSS will be found in the Bibliography, and the source of each text and significant variants are given in the Textual Notes. The poems are printed as they stand, with all inconsistencies of spelling, punctuation and layout left uncorrected.

Assembling a complete edition of a largely unpublished poet has been an exciting and enjoyable task, and I have relied on the help of many individuals, libraries and institutions, among them the late Joan Austen-Leigh; Bristol Grammar School Library; the British Library; Mary Burkett; Cambridge University Library; Tom Carpenter; Ann Channon; Roland Clare; R. Custance, Fellows' Librarian, Winchester College; David Gilson; the Hampshire Record Office; Tony Hill at Sarsen Press; the Trustees of the Jane Austen Memorial Trust; Maggie Lane; Deirdre Le Faye; Helen Lefroy; the late Derek Lucas; Michael Mangan; Allen Paterson; Andrew Shore; Brian Southam and the Committee of the Jane Austen Society; Nick Strong; University of Bristol Library Special Collections; Raymond and Roberta Warren; Freydis Welland.

I am very grateful to all of these for enabling me to make known the work of a talented poet who, if he was not quite a genius, was at least the brother of one.

DAVID SELWYN

INTRODUCTION

In 1765, the year in which James Austen was born, Samuel Johnson published his eight-volume edition of the plays of Shakespeare, with its famous Preface in which he proclaimed that the poet who held up to his readers 'a faithful mirror of manners and of life' might 'begin to assume the dignity of an ancient, and claim the privilege of established fame and prescriptive veneration'. In other words, Shakespeare was now a classic, fit to be compared with Homer and the other poets of antiquity. Fourteen years later Johnson produced the first volume of *The Lives of the Poets*, originally a venture proposed by publishers seeking to compete with an Edinburgh firm who had issued a rather inadequate *Collection of the English Poets*; Johnson was to write introductory biographies to the work of a selection of poets, chosen by the publishers rather than himself. But as he threw himself into his task the essays grew longer, and the resulting work remains a substantial and highly readable guide to late Augustan taste. It was not, perhaps, altogether the taste of the period in which it actually appeared; Johnson was seeking to preserve the centrality of the poets of the earlier part of the century, above all of Pope ('If Pope be not a poet,' he wrote, 'where is poetry to be found?'). But as with his claim for Shakespeare, the project supported the idea of a body of literature that could be considered to represent some kind of canon, an acquaintance with which might reasonably be expected of the educated reader. In an age when rampant consumerism resulted in, among other things, an enormous growth in publishing, it was inevitable that some kind of sifting process would be necessary: Dodsley's *Collection* (1748-58) and Vicesimus Knox's *Elegant Extracts in Poetry* (c.1780) are among the more successful examples; both were known to the Austen family.

Some of Johnson's opinions in *The Lives of the Poets* would not have found favour with poetry readers of the 1780s, such as James Austen. In writing about Milton he shows a certain coolness; of course he admires *Paradise Lost*, but of *Lycidas* – a poem that James knew well and which he echoed in some of his own verse – he says: '... there is no nature, for there is no truth; there is no art, for there is nothing new. Its form is that of a pastoral, easy, vulgar, and therefore disgusting: whatever images it can supply, are long ago exhausted; and its inherent improbability always forces dissatisfaction on the mind.' He concludes his attack on a poem on which he admits 'much praise has been bestowed', rather contradictorily, with the remark that 'no man could have fancied that he read *Lycidas* with pleasure, had he not known its author'. In another of the *Lives*, a poet of his own day, Thomas Gray, some of whose poetic elaborations also make themselves felt from time to time in James's style, is sternly criticised for his 'glittering accumulations of ungraceful ornaments' that 'strike, rather than please'; his images are 'magnified by affectation', his language 'laboured into harshness'. An exception is made, however, for the famous *Elegy*, in which Johnson finds genuine truth and feeling: 'Had Gray written often thus,' he says, 'it had been vain to blame, and useless to praise him.'

A poet of whom Johnson did think highly (it was at his suggestion that he was included) was James Thomson, and in this he was certainly in accord with the taste of the period. Thomson's *The Seasons*, first published complete in 1730, was an immensely successful work from the outset and it retained its popularity throughout the century and beyond. Taking as its theme the power of landscape, it encompasses a wide perspective of human experience – religious, historical, geographical, scientific; and though it looks back to Virgil and Milton, it can also be said to have anticipated, and indeed influenced, later eighteenth-century developments of the picturesque and Romanticism. It is, above all, a highly original work: Johnson rightly praised Thomson for thinking 'in a peculiar train, and ... always as a man of genius'. He 'looks round on Nature and on Life,' he wrote, 'with the eye which Nature bestows only on a poet; the eye that distinguishes, in every thing presented to its view, whatever there is on which imagination can delight to be detained, and with a mind that at once comprehends the vast, and attends to the minute. The reader of *The Seasons* wonders that he never saw before what Thomson shews him, and that he never yet has felt what Thomson impresses.' In James Austen's nature poetry the influence of Thomson can be strongly felt, not only in his language and imagery, but, in some of the longer poems, in a complexity, or perhaps rather a diffuseness of subject, that suggests that he too strove to comprehend the vast, while attending to the minute.

In the year after Johnson's death, 1785, there appeared another poem that was to have a considerable effect on James Austen (as indeed it did on Jane). This was Cowper's *The Task*; and the purpose that Cowper claimed to have in writing it – 'to recommend rural ease and leisure as friendly to the cause of piety and virtue' – might have been James's own. The gentle and precise depiction of the pleasures of country life, a practical interest in cultivation and husbandry, the love of home and the comfort of the domestic circle, an admiration for nature and the lessons it can teach, and above all an acknowledgment of the goodness and bounty of God: these are the themes of *The Task*, and they are to be found constantly in James's verse. Cowper, in fact, is arguably the poet he most closely resembles, at least in those poems that are concerned with the country; and though in some of the verses he wrote as a young man James demonstrates a capacity for fun and witty social observation, as he gets older it is the quieter pleasures of a retired country life that increasingly preoccupy him and inform his poetry. Cowper too, of course, possessed a sense of humour, and some of his poetry is very amusing; but it is the melancholy side of him that most appealed to James. Cowper had a distaste for the city and relished seclusion; James, who, apart from the nine years he spent at Oxford and a spell on the Continent, lived in Hampshire all his life, clearly identified with such feelings.

New currents were moving through poetry, however. In 1789 Blake published his *Songs of Innocence*, adding *Songs of Experience* in 1794; and in 1798 the first edition of the *Lyrical Ballads* appeared, challenging the artificiality of expression of much eighteenth-century poetry. Most of Wordsworth's greatest poems, including *The Prelude* and *The Excursion*, and all of Coleridge's, were written within James's lifetime; Byron wrote *Childe Harold's Pilgrimage*, Shelley most of *Prometheus Unbound* and Keats the *Hyperions* before his death in 1819. Yet James remained true to the spirit of Cowper and Thomson; if as he got older the word 'autumn' appeared more frequently in his work and he seemed to register with increasing frequency the inevitability of decay, it had more to do with his persistent ill health and his resigned acceptance of mortality than with any promptings of a Romantic sensibility. He was a clergyman, and a conservative one at that: under the dispensation of Providence, everyone had his proper place and was expected to remain in it, whilst acknowledging a due sense of his obligations and responsibilities to his fellow men and to his Creator; and this satisfactory state of things was not to be shaken by any radical notions expressed in what, Wordsworth called in the Preface to the Lyrical Ballads 'the language of conversation in the middle and lower classes of society'. So James Austen remained largely untouched by the shifts in poetic thought and diction that marked Romanticism's break with the eighteenth century; and in the last poem he wrote, *The Œconomy of Rural Life*, on which he was working when he died, he paid tribute to the farm bailiff at Steventon who, having saved his master's favourite colt in a fire instead of his own possessions, was taken into the rectory by James and given a home, for which he expressed eternal gratitude through 'many a year's officious service done'. As a matter of fact, there is a certain conversational quality to one or two passages in some of James's later poems that might reflect an acquaintance with Wordsworth; but it is still the phraseology and tone of his earlier models that prevail.

James Austen's literary abilities were held in high esteem by his family. Jane described him as a 'clever' man; his mother wrote of him, 'Classical Knowledge, Literary taste and the power of Elegant Composition he possessed in the highest degree'; and his son James Edward wrote in the *Memoir* that he was 'well read in English literature, had a correct taste, and wrote readily and happily, both in prose and verse'. Furthermore, when Jane Austen died in July 1817, his verse in memory of her (*see p. 86*) was copied by his brother Henry and circulated as a fitting tribute by the acknowledged family poet. Some of his other poems had already been put together into a neat group of manuscript pages (it is not known by whom); and subsequently, some dozen years after his own death, his children thought highly enough of his poetry to compile three albums of it, one presumably for each of them. Mrs Austen was of course well qualified to judge her son's writing, maternal partiality aside; she was an accomplished writer of occasional verse, and James inherited her facility with words and something of her lightness of touch. Like her, he composed ingenious riddles and charades, and verses to amuse his children (though usually to instruct them as well); and he was equally adept at seizing on a trivial domestic event – the cat sitting on a lump of dough and stopping it rising, an invitation to go out hunting – and deftly turning it into a good humoured and witty piece of verse. But he also aimed higher than that. As a well read and highly intelligent man, a clergyman for whom poetry had a moral as well as an aesthetic purpose, he naturally wished to write seriously himself; and, particularly in some of his later work, lengthy ruminations on the beauties of nature, tinged with an increasing awareness of their transience, lead him to an acceptance of human mortality, founded of course on a strong Christian faith.

It would be far from true to say, however, that his preference for the quiet pursuits of the country, as a way of life and as a theme for literature, was something that developed with increasing age and ill health. Even while he was at Oxford, the sixteen year-old boy described in his *Elegy written at Kintbury* (very much in the manner of Gray) the pleasures of walking through the water meadows by the River Kennet:

> These her loved haunts fair Solitude too calls,
> Where no rude sound her peaceful ear invades
> Save the hoarse water's din that rushing falls
> And distant murmurs from the deep cascades.   (17-20)

Contemplated from a distance, the hectic and frivolous life of the city can be thought of with a wry sense of detachment:

> Here will it oft the attentive mind amuse
> To view the maddening crowd's tumultuous strife
> Where each some glittering gew-gaw still pursues
> Thro' all the tedious hours of busy life.   (25-28)

The case for a country rather than a town life was put satirically in an essay in *The Loiterer*, the paper that James and Henry Austen published in imitation of Johnson's *Rambler* and *Idler* while they were up together at St John's College (sixty numbers were issued between January 1789 and March 1790, before James left to take up residence as curate of Overton, near Steventon). In issue No. 21, of 20 June 1789, James wrote:

> ... in spite of all the fine things which Poets, both ancient and modern, have said on the charms of Solitude, and the happiness of a Country Life, an impartial examination of the matter will convince us, that a dirty Village is not half so good a place to lounge in as the High-Street,

and that boarding at a Farmhouse is by no means so pleasant as dining
at the Cross, the Star, or the Angel.

The 'impartial examination', conducted by a lounging college Fellow setting
himself up against the accumulated wisdom of the poets of the ages, is good
robust satirical fun; and among the 'fine things' said by modem poets on the
subject of a quiet rural existence, he could have been thinking of some of his
own.

The countryside was not, however, merely a place for the passive
contemplation of the beauties of nature. Its activities, particularly its sporting
ones, were enthusiastically engaged in by James from an early age. He loved
hunting, and while he was at Oxford would ride out into the country to the
north-east on the Oxford-Bucks border for a day's sport, as he recalled years
later in *Lines written at Steventon*:

> ... in early days, a truant oft
> From Alma Mater's discipline and rule
> In spite of imposition or the frown
> Of angry Dean, or Tutor grave & wise,
> I've dashed through boggy lane and miry field
> Led by the musical and chearing notes
> Of the loud echoing pack, full many a mile.   (158-64)

Even as a curate, on an income of less than £300 a year, he kept a pack of
harriers;[1] and he hunted with the Kempshot pack and subsequently with both
William Chute's hounds from the Vyne and the Hampshire Hunt, under its
master, Truman Villebois. This was not a taste he derived from Cowper, who
fiercely denounced field sports in Book VI of *The Task*, but it was one that he
shared with his son Edward, who was equally passionate about hunting. James
was at times stricter with him than he had been with himself; while he was
preparing him for entrance to Winchester College he refused an invitation
for Edward to ride out with Mr Chute's hounds and made him stay at home
and study instead – and wrote a poem for him, to commemorate the sacrifice
(see p.67).

Much of James Austen's poetry was occasioned by particular domestic
circumstances. Most obviously this applies to the series of prologues and
epilogues that he wrote for the plays performed under his direction at
Steventon between 1782 and 1789. It had long been the habit in the theatre for
a prologue or epilogue to be provided either for a play that did not have one
by its author or where it was felt appropriate to write something specifically
for the current audience. In this way, as well as the traditional appeal for the
kindly indulgence of the spectators, a particular slant could be given to the
interpretation of what was to be, or had just been, presented, as was often the
case with the prologues and epilogues written by David Garrick. For the family
audience whom James was addressing it was hardly necessary to excuse or

apologise for the performance, though he sometimes did so with a good humoured twinkle (in the epilogue to *Matilda*, for example); and there was even less reason to attempt any manipulation of their reception of the play. But he does sometimes make a connection between play and poem by having the latter spoken specifically by one of the characters. This is particularly successful in his epilogue for *The Rivals*, which is spoken in the character of Bob Acres: James has great fun in taking the emphatic use of eccentric oaths by which Sheridan characterizes his country squire and extending it in a joyfully virtuosic display of comic bombast. The humour in these pieces is very much that of his wittier contributions to *The Loiterer*, the publication of which more or less coincided with the termination of the Steventon theatricals. He would rarely again write purely comic verse, nor indeed verse that was intended, as it were, for such 'public' exposure, except for the enigmas – verse riddles and charades – which, like all the Austens, he contributed to family games.

It is generally true to say that there is a strongly personal affection behind his poems, which are often about, and sometimes addressed to, particular people. His childhood friends the Fowles at Kintbury, and particularly Fulwar Craven, are the subject of several pieces; one of them, the *Lines written at Kintbury*, dating from his later years, is a touching elegy for members of the family who by then were dead. Naturally he wrote poems for some of the young ladies with whom, having a susceptible nature, he so easily fell in love; he certainly did not hold the view ironically expressed in *The Loiterer* that 'marrying from motives of Affection is a very improper and absurd action, injurious to our own happiness as individuals, and detrimental to the interests of the Community' (No.29). Curiously though, there is nothing dedicated to, or that even refers to, his first wife, Anne Mathew. They were married in 1792 and she died three years later. During the period of their marriage, and indeed throughout the whole childhood of their daughter Anna, James seems to have written nothing at all; at least, nothing has survived from between 1789 and 1805. The only poem that might be ascribed to those years is an entirely impersonal one, *The Maid of the Moor*, which interestingly is not included in any of the three albums, but exists only in one separate manuscript, with a watermark of 1802 (even its attribution to James is a matter of conjecture). The first piece known to be written after this long gap is, significantly, dedicated to his second wife, Mary Lloyd, and is a celebration of April, the month which contained her birthday. It is possible of course that on remarrying he destroyed anything that referred to his first marriage; but that would not explain why there is nothing from the eight years following his second; and if he had written anything for Anna, it seems unlikely that she would not have copied it into the album of his poetry that she made.

Following his resumption of poetry, almost everything he wrote was concerned with his domestic life – his wife, his two younger children and his beloved Hampshire country around Steventon, where in that same year 1805 he had succeeded his father as rector (having lived in the rectory as curate since 1801, when Mr Austen had moved with his wife and daughters to Bath). The deep love James had for his wife is expressed, after many years of marriage, in several poems; and in writing verses for Edward and Caroline, he is careful to use even the happiest occasions to teach them a beneficial lesson (his poem on Caroline's sixth birthday is perhaps the most surprising instance of this parsonical habit). As his children grew older, they too wrote poems; Edward in particular shared his father's pleasure in composition and, like him, often wrote them for other members of his family. There seems almost to have been an expectation of poetry among them. When during the autumn of 1818 rapidly failing health caused James, for a time at least, to grow tired of writing, he wrote to Caroline, who was away in Winchester at school 'Do not expect a long Poem, or any Poem upon Autumn, when you come home, –I have written quite enough in all conscience–about fading Woods and grey Skies. I do not feel as if even the present more than usually delightful Season, would extract a line from me. I suppose as I grow old, I grow dull & stupid.'[2]

In his last year, 1819, he did take up poetry again, and began *The Œconomy of Rural Life*, which, unfinished as it is, is nevertheless by far the longest and most ambitious of all his works. He also started drawing, under the influence of a young master who had been engaged for Caroline's benefit when she finally came home from school for good. While he was at Oxford James had taken drawing seriously enough to study watercolour painting with a distinguished master there, John Malchair; but as far as we know he dropped it after coming down and did not begin again until now, when he was too ill for any more active occupation. But his early studies had left him with an infallible eye and a habit of looking at landscape as if it were a painting, or as if he were himself not a poet but an artist. In passage after passage he describes natural scenery in terms of composition and lighting effects, being careful to adopt a viewpoint that would offer the best opportunity for surveying the landscape. There is no affectation in this; he is not striving for poetic effect, but attempting to interpret in verse his way of *seeing*. The opening of *Selbourne Hanger* provides one of the best examples:

> "Would you view Selbourne Hanger aright"
> You must go when Autumn's sun shines bright,
> And catches on the nearer ground;
> While from th'Horizon's utmost bound
> Some rising clouds his brighter rays
> Obscure with light and partial haze.
> 'Tis sweet on such a day as this,
> To stand upon the precipice:

And view, at first with dazzled eye,
The landscape's wild variety:
It's objects here in light displayed
There half concealed in neutral shade...
Nature itself becomes an artist, as the eye delights
                    ... distinct each part
To trace; and see with master art
How Nature works when she designs
How well each object she combines
Contrasts her forms, and breaks her lines. } (19-23)

It might be argued that this acute concentration on the artistic aspects of landscape, the poet as it were embodying the painter, is the most distinctive quality in James Austen's descriptive poetry. His style is sometimes rather predictable: although he is scrupulous in recording the precise detail of a landscape, words and phrases come round from poem to poem (as he himself implied in his letter to Caroline). Yet the verse invariably works smoothly; rhyme and scansion are meticulously adhered to, and there is invariably a clear sense of form and direction. Above all, an unmistakable voice emerges from the poetry as a whole: wise, intelligent, humane, and when addressing his children in particular, audibly individual. The interest in reading James's poetry is bound to be primarily biographical, but there are many incidental delights; and at his best, as in perhaps the two poems about Caroline's cat Tyger, he can stand comparison with any writer of light verse of his day.

Notes

1 See Mary Augusta Austen Leigh, *James Edward Austen Leigh: a memoir* (1911), p.14.
2 HRO 23M93/MI fiche 123 f.44[3].

An Epistle to Fulwar Craven Fowle Esqr.
supposed Secretary of State in the reign of Geo: 4th
by J^s. Austen as a Country Curate

While you my Friend, with titles crowned
Tread busy life's fatiguing round;
    While the loud voice of Fame,
Where e're his tide old Ocean pours
'Gainst barbarous nation's distant shores
    Spreads far & wide your name;

Can'st Thou awhile thy brow unbend
And deign with pleasure to attend
    His unaffected Lays,
Who, pleased thy growing worth to see,   10
First tuned the Doric reed for thee
    To celebrate thy praise?

Remember well thou can'st I ween,
Each tranquil hour, each happy scene,
    Which we were wont to taste;
When we no other pleasure sought,
No joys remote, or dearly bought
    In our own converse blest.

Together often have we strayed
Thro' many a daisy-dappled mead,   20
    And flower-enamelled vales;
Or haply thro' some leafy grove
Caught the soft plainings of the dove,
    Who her lost mate bewails.

By Phœbus hotter beams when tired,
Together oft have we retired
    To some wood-fringed retreat;
Where the time beaten willow shoots
Thro' the worn banks it's tangled roots
    For Naïds trim the seat.   30

1

Oft were we wont in such recess,
When disencumbered of all dress,
    To stem the adverse tide;
With open arms the wave embrace,
The wave, that to our arms gave place,
    When gently thrown aside.

But when the dog-star's fiercer beams
Retire, & Autumn pours his streams
    O'er every misty vale,
High on the uplands when the morn   40
First echoes to the Hunter's horn
    We met the piercing gale.

When winter came with look profound
To crown the variegated round,
    And close the circling year;
When by the blasts of Eurus keen
Dismantled of their livery green
    The leafless woods appear:

When frosts that rise, & winds that pierce
And snows descending foul & fierce   50
    Forbade the sylvan toil;
The genial feast we'd then prolong;
With festive mirth and jocund song
    The weary hours beguile.

What though those days can ne'er return
Twere folly sure for that to mourn;
    'Twere wise to be content;
With what the Gods to us allow,
And thank them with unclouded brow,
    For all their blessings sent.   60

To different men the fates assign
A different part to act; 'twas thine,
    To bask in glory's blaze;
Twas mine to woo in lowly strain
The nymphs of fountain, wood or plain
    To bless my peaceful lays.
          Æt: 15

2

An Elegy
written at Kintbury Berks, addressed to FCF.

Amid the temperate hours of evening grave,
Oft was I wont in thoughtful mood to stray,
Where Kennet's crystal stream with limpid wave
Thro' Kintbury's meadows takes it's winding way.
Full oft amid the solemn gloom of night,
When thick descending falls the balmy dew,
When Cynthia's silver lamp darts paler light
Along it's banks my path would I pursue.

There shadowy forms unnumbered oft arise,
And lightly tripping o'er the mossy green   10
Noted by fancy's visionary eyes
In various shapes, & mystic forms are seen.
There Contemplation too, sweet placid maid,
Beneath a shell-framed grotto lies behind
In simple state of virgin white arrayed
Her auburn locks loose floating to the wind.

These her loved haunts fair Solitude too calls,
Where no rude sound her peaceful ear invades
Save the hoarse water's din that rushing falls
And distant murmurs from the deep cascades.   20
Save that from yonder oak-crowned airy steep
Where the dank grass & tufted weeds among
The gothic Abbey's mould'ring ruins peep,
The night bird screams her melancholy song.

Here will it oft the attentive mind amuse
To view the maddening crowd's tumultuous strife
Where each some glittering gew-gaw still pursues
Thro' all the tedious hours of busy life.
While these with pomp & glitter struck, delight
With toilsome painful steps, & marches slow,   30
To gain Ambition's frail & tottering height
And stand conspicuous to the crowd below.

With unremitting zeal the Pedant sage
While his dim lamp consumes the midnight oil
Turns o'er the dusty folio's antique page
Nor dreams his labour ought but pleasing toil.
No wave's wild war the careful Merchant fears,
When to the winds he spreads his swelling sails,
Intent on gain he inattentive hears
The winds that hoarsely blow in rougher gales.   40

Not so the Miser, he with look profound
Less than his dashing gold regarding rest
Takes e're he sleeps each night his wonted round
And views wth. anxious eyes his wealth-confining chest.
How large the Crew that shunning business' round
In genial feasts expand the joyous soul;
Anacreon-like their brows with myrtle crowned
When stretched at ease they drain th'inspiring bowl.

His fond pursuit let each one then enjoy
Nor er'e shall I with envy view their fate   50
Whilst solid bliss that ne'er can cloy
Thro' life's retired vale my steps await
Place me in farthest Scythia's trackless waste,
Where no fair prospect the dull way beguiles,
Whose dreary hills no sweets of summer taste
No vintage reddens, & no harvest smiles;.

Yet with thy converse blest each gloomy scene
Each desert hill a fertile look would wear,
And the east wind that o'er the waste howls keen
Should to my partial sense a zephyr mild appear.   60

Æt.16

The Hermit

1

Beneath yon oak-crowned hill whose solemn shades
In prospect wild o'er hang the vale beneath
From whose romantic glooms, & twilight glades
Luxuriant flowers their grateful odours breathe;
Well known to Nymphs who twine the fragrant wreath,
When Maia's sweets the vernal showers disclose,
When the wild thyme embalms the furzy heath
And in the clovered dale the cowslip blows
And through the garden's maze the sweetly blushing rose.

2

Beneath this hill, I ween, an ancient Sage,   10
Within the windings of a vaulted cell,
Whose silver hairs attest his reverend age,
As old tradition goes, long time did dwell;
The village swains & nymphs all knew him well;
Content within this Cave would he reside,
Here oft turned o'er Religion's sacred page;
Of simple mien was he, nor ought allied
To the dull prosing sons of Pedantry & Pride.

3

Midst the still pleasures of retired life,
In gentle lapse his moments slid away,   20
All undisturbed by tumult, noise, or strife,
Calm as the sunshine of a summer's day,
When rural nymphs spread out the tedded hay,
His time nor flew too fast, nor lagged too slow,
Nor when beneath the Dog-star's parching ray,
Nor when the trees all stand in leafless row,
And winter's piercing blasts bring down the drifted snow.

4

Full oft when o'er yon beechen tufted hill
With ruddy streaks the dappled east first gleams,
When his diurnal journey to fulfill,   30
The rising sun first darts his glowing beams,
And gilds the distant vales & silver streams;
Oft when the returning radiance bright

Had chased away the morning's airy dreams,
Would he ascend yon Mountain's shrubby heigth
And greet with thankful heart the sun's returning light.

5

There stopping oft along the mountain's side,
Pleased would he view the glittering prospect round,
Where the near fertile plains extended wide,
And distant hills with ripening harvest crowned   40
Or leafy foliage decked, the prospect bound;
Or where the brooks their wild waves wandering lead
Thro' vales responsive to the vocal sound
Of the shrill oaten pipe, & pastoral reed,
Well tuned by swains whose flocks those meadows feed.

6

But when the morning fogs are chased away,
And melt before the sun's superior power,
When from high Heaven he darts his dazzling ray,
Shunning the hotness of the noon tide hour,
To yonder banks where eglantines embower   50
With their umbrageous leaves a mossy seat,
And shelter give to many a modest flower
That shuns the powerful sun's all conquering heat,
With book in hand well pleased would he retreat.

7

When to fair Thetis arms the sun retires,
And all the west with glittering purple dyes,
When the rooks clamour from the village spires,
When thro' the Vale the evening mists arise,
And with their dusky clouds o'erhang the skies,
When home returning from the fertile plains   60
To his thatched Cot the swain all chearful hies,
There with a homely meal rewards his pains,
And Monarch of his smiling cottage reigns.

8

Where the wild cliffs entangled craggy steeps
Re echo to the brook that brawls along
It's rocky channel, or still murmuring creeps,
Where Philomel all sad proclaims her wrong,

6

In faintly warbled notes, a plaintive song,
In thoughtful silence often would he stray
The matted grass, & trembling reeds among,   70
With grateful heart would frame the sacred lay
To him whose goodness great does all our pains o'er pay.

9

So passed his time when spring her vesture throws
O'er every verdant hill & flowery mead:
But when the earth beneath the Dog-star glows,
When the faint drooping flocks forget to feed,
And their tired shepherd too lays by his reed;
Then listless he his weary length reclines
Where from the parching ray securely freed,
To the calm powers of sleep his sense resigns   80
Beneath the cooling shade of Beech or waving Pines.

10

When Autumn's blast the pensive wood bereaves
Of all the verdure which their branches crowned,
And thro' the grove the sadly faded leaves
Fall in a yellow shower with rustling sound
Or in dry heaps lie scattered o'er the ground;
When now no more melodious warblings float
The windings of the leafless grove around,
Save that the Red Breast strains his little throat,
And from the tufted Cot still pours an artless note.   90

11

Then to his Cot content would he retire,
There refuge find from each intruding care,
Would heap fresh fuel on the evening fire
And with his friends the rural banquet share,
Pitied the great, & blest his homely fare;
Then the still listening crowd would he advise
Against Life's adverse changes to prepare,
Shew them that happiness in virtue lies,
And teach them worldly pleasures to despise.

12

Here let not then the censuring sons of Pride,   100
Who the calm sweets of quiet life ne'er knew,

7

His simple mien & manners pure deride,
Nor let the vain with scornful mockery view
The charms which from fair Nature's source he drew,
Nor let the critic blame the humble lays
Of him who paints such worth in numbers true,
That he attempts his measure weak to raise
And give to modest worth it's just deserved praise.

Æt. 16.

Prologue to the Tragedy of Matilda,
acted at Steventon Hants.
Spoken by Edward Austen

When Thespis first professed the mimic. art,
Rude were his Actors, & his stage a cart;
No scene gay painted, to the eye displayed
The waving honours of the sylvan glade:
No canvass Palace pleased the wondering sight,
No rosined lightening flashed its forked light;
No iron bowl the rolling thunder forms,
No rattling pease proclaim the driving storms;
No glittering falchion graced the Hero's side,
No nodding feathers rose in tinselled pride;   10
No angry Monarch vowing vengeance loud,
Pleased with his full mouthed rant the list'ning crowd
T'was simple nature then they kept in view,
Thence well earned plaudits from their audience drew
Far other figure wears our modern Stage,
The wise improvement of this happier age.
Far other scenes the British Stage demands,
And force th'applause of sticks, canes, feet & hands.
When by his Rival's tin her lover dies
The Lady first with cambric wipes her eyes,   20
Then backwards falling (whilst her slave with pain
Adjusts the drapery of her rumpled train)
In desperate rage her beauteous tresses tears,
By different fits scolds, prays, cries, raves & swears;

Then gently falling on her Lover's breast,
In quiet slumbers sinks at last to rest.
Tears from each eye this scene pathetic draws,
And critic galleries loudly shout applause.
    At once our audience to instruct & please,
To speak with elegance, & act with ease,   30
To fill the softened soul with grief sincere,
And draw from pity's eye the tender tear;
These are the triumphs of the tragic lyre –
To this, though far unequal we aspire,
And fondly hope from your applause to gain.
A great reward for all our care & pain –
                                              Æta 17

Epilogue to the Tragedy of Matilda
spoken by Mr T. Fowle.

Halloo! Good Gentlefolks! What none asleep!
And could you really your attention keep
To a dull tale, which passed the Lord knows when,
Touched up too by a vulgar Parson's pen?
And you fair Ladies too, what silent all!
Not one word spoke of Opera, Play, or Ball?
Olympian dew, or Essence for the face,
Of cheapening Milliners, or washing lace;
A hen-pecked Husband, or a broken fan,
Nor one soft whisper to the charming man!   10
To say the truth, we all affronted feel,
Such usage is nor proper nor Genteel.
To tread the stage at all at first we feared,
But'twas some comfort if we were not heard.
At your applause we were astonished quite,
Matilda's hardly yet o'er come her fright.
Why what d'ye think your neighbours all will say?
I fear they'll think you came to see the Play.
Which, except love between a man & wife,
Is really the most vulgar thing in life,   20
Jesting apart, we here can only say,
'Tis ours with due civility to pay
Our grateful thanks for this attention shewn;

Nor can we quite ourselves desertless own,
Since your applause this evening sure decrees
Some share of merit in the wish to please.

Æta I7.

Prologue to The Rivals –
Acted by some young Ladies & Gentlemen at Steventon
Spoken by H. Austen. July 1784

Once more my friends, by youthful fancy led,
With bold but cautious step the stage we tread;
And, of your partial praise perhaps too vain.
Once more the same indulgence hope to gain.
Let woe worn grief, or hoary age admire
The loftier numbers of the tragic Lyre;
Court the soft pleasures that from pity flow;
Seek joy in tears & luxury in woe,.
'Tis ours, less noble, not less pleasing task,
To draw from folly's features fashion's mask;   10
To paint the scene where wit & sense unite
To yield at once instruction & delight;
Where lively mirth with innocence combines,
Where wit's keen shaft fair decency refines.
'Tis ours to show true virtue's image dres't
In the light drapery of Fancy's vest;
To teach gay youth, which glows at pleasure's name
That virtue's path & pleasure's are the same.
Ye blooming Fair, from whose propitious smile,
We hope a sweet reward for all our toil,   20
Though yet too young your stronger power to own,
We fondly wait your smile, & dread your frown.
Smile but this evening, & in riper years,
When manhood's strength has damp'd our boyish fears,
Our hearts, with genuine grace & beauty caught,
In fervent sighs, shall thank you as they ought.
You'll see us suppliants at your feet again,
And they who liked as Boys shall love as Men.

Epilogue to the Rivals

Though I've hardly recovered myself from the fright
Odds tremors! which rose at that Beverley's sight;
Yet the Epilogue still I dare venture to speak,
For my lungs are as strong as my courage is weak,
Nor shall it in Devonshire ever be said,
Little Bob stood abashed, in the country though bred,
Or was ever his person afraid to display,
By my valour! when fire arms are not in the way.
And his greatest of enemies surely must own,
That both valour & conduct are here to be shewn,   10
Since bright eyes worse than swords can kill, murder, & slay
And the aim can destroy tho' the pistol's away.
Nor, odds Blunders & Balls! c^d. Sir Lucius e're dare
With such weapons his Counsellor e're to compare.
And here let me put in a word of advice,
Odds Counsels! & then I'll have done in a trice.
When the Loves & the Graces all sport in y^r. mien
When low at y^r. feet the fond Lover is seen
When, odds Fuels & Flames! he assures you he burns,
And humbly solicits the smallest returns,   20
Sir Lucius's plan is the best on my word;
Let your wit be as polished though keen as his sword,
Let your eyes whose least frown w^d. his comfort destroy
Odds Lustres! give loose to his torrent of joy!

The Rash Resolution
to
Miss Austen

1

As fair Eliza t'other day
Forgetting for a while her play
Leant o'er her Brother's chair
She mark'd his face with look profound
Saw scraps of paper scrawled around
His brow perplex'd with care

2

Curious the latent cause to find
Which thus to Poetry inclin'd
    A Youth of vacant head
She rashly vows her weary Eyes
Sleeps stealing power shall ne'er surprise
    Till she those lines has read

      10

3

Exerting therefore all the power
Which to subdue our tempers sour
    Fate gave to Woman's brain
With all the Eloquence of eyes
Her Brothers heart to move she tries
    But tries Alas! in vain

4

With Sorrow I my tale pursue
Ah! what can poor Eliza do
    For Night comes on apace
Studious her half clos'd eyes to keep
Safe from the numbing Power of Sleep
    She moves from place to place

      20

5

In vain, for by the listless nod
I see too plain the potent God
    His poppies soon will shed;
Yes, yes, I see he has her fast,
Here, here, good Betty, hither haste,
    And carry her to Bed.

      30

6

'Twas morn, and round the Breakfast Board
With every wholesome viand stored
    The youthful circle prest
Eliza shunned her Brother's look
But her soft hand he smiling took,
    And thus the Nymph address'd.

7

"Will my Dear Sister pleas'd peruse
"The efforts of an humble Muse
"Nor blame the homely Style?
"Then with what appetite you may 40
"Proceed to take your Dejeuné
"And bless us with her smile.

8

"Yet, yet, but one short minute hold
And quick the paper I'll unfold
"Which holds the wish'd for Prize,
"Mean while I give you this short hint,
"Which in your bosom deep imprint,
"Then feast your longing Eyes.

9

"Your curiosity restrain,
"It may be done, tho' done with Pain, 50
"No rash resolves e're make:
"Sink in your mind this lesson deep,
"They may be very hard to keep,
"But easy still to break.

10

"So may each charm your steps attend,
"Which Beauty Grace & ease can send,
"To make you please through Life;
"May you to some fond Youth be join'd
"Who in your Form alone can find
"The blessings of a Wife. 60

J.A: June 24th – 84

13

Sonnet to Lady Catherine Powlet

Spring Wood! thy verdant walks well pleased I view;
Whether the morn's bright radiance streak the skies,
Or from the vale the evening mists arise,
And tinge the Landscape with a dusky hue;
Along thy walks my path will I pursue,
And view thy beauties with unwearied eyes;
Mark thy wild foliage with its various dyes;
The oak's bright green, the waving poplar's blue.
Thou fair Idalic's love-devoted shades,
Thou the famed charms of Paphos blooming grove   10
No more shall envy, since their glory fades,
No longer haunted by the Queen of Love;
Who now a mortal, round thy happier glades
In lovely Catherine's form delights to rove.

Sonnet to Winter

Stern Monarch of the howling tempests hail!
Welcome fierce Winter, with thy gloomy train,
Dank mists, keen frosts, or quick descending rain,
Or snows white sweeping down each drifted dale.
What though thy tyrant blasts my cot assail,
My rush-fringed brook with torrent floods distain
Though thy chill forests it's icy waves enchain
Or o'er the woodland throw thy kirtle pale;
Yet well I know what sports thy hours beguile,
When the young circle round the blazing hearth   10
With gambols deft, or mazy wanton wile
Drown the loud storm in louder bursts of mirth,
When beauty decked in many a witching smile
And music's power to gentle Love give birth

Sonnet to Spring

Parent of winning smiles & soft desires,
Youth of the opening year! haste genial Spring!
Quick urge thy doubtful steps, & with thee bring
What e're Love's sweetly pleasing pain inspires,
What ere the bashful maid's coy bosom fires,
Oer whom the Idalian Boy with purple wing
Fluttering, his magic chains essays to fling,
And bind that breast where Innocence retires.
Thee Spring I bless, not that thy blooming scene,
The dying softness of the western breeze,   10
The lightly waving tints of varying green
Alone with joy my ravish'd senses seize;
But that thy influence o'er my Fair one's mien
Gives some faint dawnings of my passion's ease.

Sonnet to Autumn

Nymph of the straw-crowned hat, & kirtle pale,
Mild Autumn come, & cheer thy longing Swain;
Whether thou pleased survey'st the yellow plain
Bend in light currents to the western gale;
Or from yon mountain's summit view'st the vale
Now dim with fogs, now dank with mizzling rain,
Or warn'st collected on the village Fane,
Light summer's guests to spread their plumy sail
Sweet season welcome, for nor Summer's blaze,
Spring's vernal sweets, nor Winter's tempests wild   10
Like thy soft scenes invite my willing Lays,
When 'neath thy tranquil sky serene & mild,
I frame light measures in my Fair one's praise
Or muse, lone Melancholy's favoured child.

15

Sonnet to Summer

Veiled in thy radiant vest of streaming light,
Whilst midst thy parted locks soft zephyrs play,
Fair Summer come, & bring the lengthened day,
The dewy evening, & the milder night;
With many a fair returning morning bright,
With many a dazzling noon prolong thy stay,
Nor from these plains too eager haste away,
Quick to the southern climes to wing thy flight.
So shall our blessings still thy steps attend,
So shall the humble tenants of the plain,   10
Whilst o'er their floated meads the rains descend
Whilst torrent floods their woodland scenes distain,
Warmed by thy smiles submissive learn to bend
Beneath dark Autumn's sway, or Winter's tyrant reign.

1785

Sonnet
on leaving Oxford in the evening May 14th 1785

What fondly cherish'd thoughts my bosom-fill,
As yon dark mansions from my sight retire,
As the last turret black & pointed spire
Vanish, slow sinking 'neath the far seen hill,
While half hushed murmurs from the distant mill
The white smoke rising from the village fire,
Wake in my breast such social soft desire,
And thoughts of Home into my heart instill.
Thus fondly wrapt in Fancy's magic dream
And many a Castle forming, on I stray   10
Cross the lone heath, or deeper shaded dale,
While soft reflected in the wavy stream
Night's full orbed Queen directs my dubious way
Tinting the woodlands round with radiance pale.

Lines
Addressed to Miss Charlotte Brydges

Why beats my heart with fear oppre'st,
Why droops my soul with woe forlorn,
Why from my pillow gentle rest
Fly'st thou before th' approach of morn?
Why last, er'e yet my Eyelids close,
Must – – power my bosom feel,
Or why, midst morns disturbed repose
Her fair form o'er my Fancy steal?
Say, is it love my bosom fires?
Much, much I fear least such it prove.   10
Yes, by these tremors, Hopes, Desires
I fear, I know, I feel 'tis Love.
Then Oh farewell ye joyous days;
At once adieu ye nights of ease?
For if my heart Love's power obeys
I hope not happiness or peace.
Shall I attempt the Nymph to gain
For whom a thousand Lovers die,
Or hope she can relieve my pain
When she can never hear me sigh?   20
Distressed, perplexed, 'twixt hope & fear
My days unheeded slide along,
I know not how my bark to stear
And while I doubt am doubly wrong.
Thus, 'twixt two rocks, whose rugged height
Frowns sullen o'er the foaming Tide,
The Pilot seized with pale affright
Can neither way his vessel guide.

Sonnet to the same

Sweet maid, whose opening charms as morning fair
Unnumbered hearts in silent sorrows own;
Whose voice is music in it's sweetest tone,
Say, how in measure meet shall I declare
What varying pasions my sad bosom tear -
Say, in what words shall I my flame make known

17

For thou who gav'st the wound can'st tell alone
The fiereceness of a pang too keen to bear.
And, oh instruct me by what act to gain
From those dear lips the so much wish'd reply.   20
Is that too much? and am I doomed in vain
For ever doomed to heave the hopeless sigh?
Teach me not then to bear a load of pain,
But teach me, sweet Enchantress, how to die!

supposed to have been written about 1786.

Prologue to The Wonder.
Acted at Steventon Decr. 28th: & 29th: 1787

Let Spring his green & rosy wreath display,
Let dazzling Summer boast her lengthen'd day;
From his full horn let ruddy Autumn pour
The viny clusters, or the grainy store;
Their charms, to others I with ease resign,
But be the social joys of Christmas mine.
T'is thine alone fair season to impart
A genial glow to every human heart:
Thy presence gives to wit & fancy birth,
And warms the coldest breast to social mirth.   10
To thee, from old, what festive joys belong!
Thine was the Bard's Romance, & Minstrel's song.
Nor less in later times thy solemn rites,
When Britain's gentle Dames & peerless Knights
In due obedience to thy annual call,
Assembled cheerful in the Baron's Hall.
Then many a trick, & many a gambol neat,
And many a frolic, helped the time to cheat.
Nor yet in lov'd Eliza's golden reign
Did Christmas ever claim its rites in vain.   20
Imported from the mirthful shores of France,
They trod with awkward steps the formal dance
Then bearded Lords met ruff encircled Fair,
And moved in tawdry Pageants pair by pair;
While led by Leicester through the opening crowd,

Alike of policy & beauty proud,
Distinguished both by ugliness & dress,
First of the brilliant troop, march'd great Queen Bess.
But soon alas! these joys were doomed to cease,
And mirth left Britain's Isle with sense & peace.   30
Then came a set of men, with formal faces,
Ranting quotations wild, with strange grimaces.
To smirk was then a sign of rebrobation,
To smile was sinful, but to laugh, damnation.
They could High Treason in plum porridge spy,
And smelled plain Popery in a Christmas pie.
For ten long years the nation groaned & sighed,
And the men ranted while the women cried.
At length with shame each British bosom burned,
And Charles, & loyalty & wit returned;   40
Mirth with the Monarch reassumed her reign,
And Christmas wore her usual smile again.
Since this, when'ere the rustic holly's seen
To deck the window with its sober green,
For festive joys each youthful mind prepares,
And age almost forgets his pains & cares;
And whilst their sports his vigour half restore,
He counts the gambols of his youth once more.
This night, though not with pain, at least with care,
To please our friends a trifle we prepare,   50
And if in the attempt we miss our aim
Indulgence by prescriptive right we claim.
Then pass upon our faults a censure light,
And smile upon the gambols, of this night.

Epilogue to the Comedy of The Wonder,
acted at Steventon 26th: & 28th: Decr: 1787
Spoken by a Lady in the character of Violante.

In barbarous times, e'er learning's sacred light
Rose to disperse the shades of Gothic night
And bade fair science wide her beams display,
Creation's fairest part neglected lay.
In vain the form, where grace & ease combined,
In vain the bright eye spoke th'enlightened mind,
In vain the sweet smiles which secret love reveal,
Vain every charm, for there were none to feel.
From tender childhood trained to rough alarms,
Losing no music but the clang of arms;   10
Enthusiasts only in the listed field,
Our youth then knew to fight, but not to yield.
Nor higher deemed of beauty's utmost power,
Than the light plaything of their idler hour.
Such was poor woman's lot – whilst tyrant men
At once possessors of the sword & pen
All female claim, with stern pedantic pride
To prudence, truth & secresy denied,
Covered their tyranny with specious words,
That called themselves creation's mighty Lords –   20
But thank our happier stars, those days are o'er,
And woman holds a second place no more.
Now forced to quit their long held usurpation,
These men all wise, these Lords of the Creation!
To our superior rule themselves submit,
Slaves to our charms, & vassals to our wit.
We can with ease their every sense beguile,
And melt their resolutions with a smile.
To us each various rank its homage pays,
Nor must that poet hope for lasting praise,   30
Who twines not myrtle with his wreath of bays.
To crown her sex with well deserved applause,
(A female champion in a female cause)
This night's gay Authoress her pen employed,
Nor is the lively tale of moral void,
Since Lovers, nay & Husbands, hence may know,
That jealousy is ever love's worst foe.
That he must surely act the wisest part,

Who gives his faith where he has given his heart,
That confidence must ever mutual prove   40
And tie in closer knots the rosy bands of love.

Prologue to *The Chances*.
Acted at Steventon Jan^y: 1788

In those sad times, which once Britannia knew,
When few gave Balls, & no one played at Loo;
When children loved their Parents, men their wives,
And spent in dull domestic joys their lives,
How stiff the monsters walked, how starched they dres't,
And scarce less starched the doctrines they professed
They taught their children virtue, sense & truth,
And tainted thus the minds of tender youth;
Told the poor things such heaps of horrid lies,
That happiness was ever virtue's prize –   10
That e'en amusement should some good provide
And wait, instruction's handmaid, at her side.
But chiefly told them, (to their lasting shame) –
"My children, above all things, never game".
From rules like these, what good could one expect
Their precepts took indeed a sad effect:
Their stupid sons were ready to adore 'em,
And lived as virtuous as their Sires before 'em –
But ye my friends, who live in happier times,
Blush not too deeply at your Father's crimes   20
'Tis true I own, in spite of all our care,
We cannot but remember, "Such things were".
But hard indeed & wretched were our case,
Could not our merits all their faults efface.
Since we (nor can our foes deny the boast)
Have spared nor industry, nor care, nor cost,
To throw at once their Gothic fabric down,
And on their system's ruins, build our own.
Hail happy times! hail halcyon days of mirth!
When pleasure courts us from our very birth.   30
No more shall prudence, with her chilling powers,
Blast every joy that blooms in youth's gay bowers
Duty no more 'gainst pleasure war shall wage,

21

Nor indiscretion fear the frown of age,
Since fashion's magic power, through this wise nation,
Has so completely changed each rank & station,
That they who guide the plough, or guide the state,
The important little, & the vulgar great,
Young men of threescore, & old men of one,
Alike to dissipation's Temple run,   40
And high & low, all say, or seem to say,
The first, the greatest joy of life, is play. –
Come here my son, (the titled Gamester cries)
My precepts mark, & thou in life shal't rise;
For happy child! for thou shalt near be beaten
By pedants harsh, at Winchester or Eton.
Let vulgar children all their letters know –
Two are for thee sufficient – E & O –
Into the fire let other books be hurled,
Read thou one book, and be that book, the world.   50
Hence armed completely, midst thine equals go –
Consider every man thou meet'st thy foe.
"Pay where you must, & cheat wher'ere you can,
The proper plunder of mankind is man".
Instructed thus our youth makes quick advances;
Throws Lilly's grammar by, & learns the chances.
O'er Hoyle & Paine all day intent he pours,
And cheats his Father's footmen at all fours.
At college shines in every knowing set,
And ends all disputation with a bet.   60
Then in some gambling Club obtains a seat,
And grows e're twenty one, a rogue complete.
But soft – we must not now be too severe,
For we alas! ourselves are Gamesters here,
And deep ones too – we stake our reputation
To gain, if fortune smile, your approbation;
And though in truth against long odds we try,
Yet we will stand the hazard of the die. –

Prologue to the Tragedy of Tom Thumb. –
Acted to a small circle of select friends,
& spoken by the Author.
March 22ᵈ: 1788

In every clime where science spreads her reign,
In ever lively France, or sluggish Spain,
Mids't generous Britains, or ungenerous Dutch,
Mids't those who save too little or too much,
Though jarring politics distract them quite,
Though feeble treaties do but half unite,
How'ere unlike their other systems be,
In one grand system all for once agree;
Consenting all this leading maxim own,
That pleasure reigns man's great concern alone;   10
And though each various race, each different clime,
May have their favourite modes of killing time,
Pleasure, of all exists the common aim;
The means may vary, the intent the same.
Through all the wide extent of laughing France,
How madly gay the merry beggars dance!
Thrice happy race! your mirth's exhaustless store
Much I admire, but praise your patience more,
Who, while each various ill your country threats,
Of private poverty, & public debts,   20
Whils't Britains Fleet o'erhangs your humbled shore,
Whilst Farmers general torment you more,
Wisely in scenes of mirth your time employ –
Practise your steps, & halloo "Vive le Roi" –
Ne'er can your woes be of resource bereft,
Whils't you've one single yard of catgut left.
In Spain, where half oppressed by his own weight,
Pride's haughty genius reigns in listless state,
E'en there amusement claims one annual day,
And almost teaches Spaniards to be gay.   30
Then fired with hope, each Hero from afar,
Speeds to the capital of fall'n Navarre;
Dressed for the fight, each noble Butcher stands,
The long knife quivering in his eager hands,
And great the joy, through Pampelune's proud walls,
When, struck with nicest art the monster falls.
Pleased with the noble deed, the exulting crowd

Resound his praise with acclamations loud,
While from the window's height, with kind regard,
His mistress looks a far more sweet reward. 40
In Holland too, whose dull & tasteless sons,
Might claim the glorious name of modern Huns,
Whose mental fogs no ray of genius breaks,
Dull as their skies, & muddy as their lakes;
Though all seems wrapt in one surrounding gloom,
And business for amusement scarce leaves room,
Pleasure e'en here one fainter effort makes,
And the dull Nation at her touch awakes –
Warmed by the genial heat which gin supplies
They brave the keen blast of December's skies 50
With arms close crossed, or wide on kimbo spread,
Pipes in their mouths & night caps on their head,
They skim the smooth canal's new frozen plain,
And soothe their minds with hopes of future gain.
But chief in this, our Heaven protected land,
Where wealth & liberty walk hand in hand
Through all our cultured fields or rocky coasts,
A numerous train of votaries pleasure boasts.
On us her varied gifts the Goddess flings,
And each new day a new enjoyment brings: 60
Her form each hour assumes a different hue,
Like rainbows shifting to the gazer's view.
When Summer throws from his meridian height,
O'er fainting worlds a stream of dazzling light,
Beneath the burning heats of August's sun,
On the parched downs, like men stark mad we run.
With eyes intent the striker's motion watch,
The swift struck ball with smarting fingers catch.
With eager joys our fluttering bosoms beat,
And pleasure then is toil, fatigue & heat. 70
In winter, 'ere the morn yet glows with red,
Though scarcely half awake we leave our bed;
Forth to th'appointed wood with joy repair,
Nor heed the damps of raw November's air -
With manly hearts our sufferings we deride,
And freeze & shiver by the Covert's side;
Cheered by the rattling crash & screaming halloo,
O'er clayey vales & flinty Hills we follow;
Pant o'er the Common field's low level plains,

Strain up steep banks, & plunge through boggy lanes,   80
Each animated heart the scene enjoys,
And finds true bliss in danger, dirt & noise.
At eve returned from these bewitching sports,
A stiller scene of joy our presence courts.
Then down we sit, the happy chosen four,
Eye the rich stakes, & careful keep the score:
Oft with our partner's blunders find great fault,
Rub our own heads, & look as if we thought:
Then slap the table with a thump so hard,
You'd swear our all was placed upon that card;   90
But if the circle small this bliss denies,
The chequered board its ready help supplies
There, ranged on either side with nicest care,
Two rival powers for dreadful war prepare.
With looks intent, across the board we bend,
Attack with vigour, or with care defend;
Unmindful how the waning night steals on,
And start surprised to hear the clock strike one.
Delightful game! you of all pastimes most,
Over each sex resistless power may boast,   100
Since Britain's fair your influence confess,
And leave the unfinished work, to play at chess.
Such are the sports of Britain's happy days,
Each has its charm, & each alternate sways:
Each singly powerless life's cold hours to warm,
Draws from society its dearest charm.
Then let not taste, with critic eye severe
View the light scenes which we exhibit here.
Let not the judgment keen of riper age,
Mock the small Hero of our infant stage.   110
Though small indeed the Hero of to-night,
He can, like other Heroes, love & fight;
Can sigh in sentiment, in passion roar,
And Philip's son himself did little more.
For him who thus, (your goodness not unknown)
Stands forth his comrade's champion, & his own
Whose pencil rude has some strange groups pourtrayed
In a rough outline, which he could not shade,
Who thus, with greater zeal than care defines
His bosom's feelings in these artless lines;   120
To please no numerous crowd he e'er pretends –

He writes & lives but for his private friends.
Their vacant hours to amuse, his favourite toil,
And his best thanks are their approving smile –

Prologue to a private *Theatrical Exhibition at Steventon.*
1788

Well sings the Bard of Britain's happier age,
All men are players, all the world a stage;
And were we but to search this Kingdom through
We soon should find the bold assertion true.
Hence high & low, the fair sex & the brave,
The Monarch's courtier, & the courtier's slave,
All speak a language foreign to their hearts,
And each one in his time plays many parts.
And if, our real opinion to conceal,
To talk of feeling, when we do not feel,   10
If this be acting, sure in scenic powers
No age, no nation ever rivalled ours –
The simpering courtiers first the Scene begin,
Anxious by smoothest words our praise to win:
They much extol our riches, power & strength,
In periods neatly turned of measured length:
Praise the successful schemes themselves have planned,
And scatter cornucopiae through the land,
With magic power make wars & taxes cease,
And talk of nought but harmony & peace.   20
Not so the country Squire – rough, honest, stern,
His breast for public good alone can burn;
He no distinction makes t'wixt Whig & Tory,
A friend to English beef & English glory.
He wishes Ministers were clear & plain,
Such as they were in good Queen Bess's reign,
And not amuse a poor deluded nation,
With the vain pomp of flimsy declamation.
The courtier's schemes he cruelly cuts short,
And gives him the uncourteous retort,   30
Nor more respects his plans for wealth & power,
Than Hotspur did the Devil of Glendower.
Amidst such doubts, what plan shall we pursue,

Perplexed the Labyrinth, but short the clue.
And soon this truth we readily shall trace –
The one is in, the other out of place.
Now quit the comic Scenes of public strife,
And let us view the Farce of private life;
And we shall find amongst all ranks & stations,
Such plots, such denouements & transformations,   40
That even envys self must grant us merit,
And own we act our parts with care & spirit.
Observe yon Lover, in devotion warm,
Praising Miss Prudence Plum's lean haggard form,
See with what zeal his ardent suit he presses,
For well he knows what charms his fair possesses;
Her freeholds, copyholds – has marked them all,
And longs her India Bonds his own to call.
Nay I *have* heard – not that I think it fact,
That man & wife have each their part to act,   50
That when the pair on life's grand scene appear,
Then every word is Love, & Life & Dear –
But the house empty & the curtain down,
Husbands can storm, & gentle wives can frown.
But far from us such gross insinuations;
We ne'er attack our neighbour's reputations,
Too happy if your candour will to-night
View our own Actors in the fairest light;
In spite of criticism's rigid laws,
Our light & trifling exhibition draws,   60
The grateful tribute of our friends' applause. –

Epilogue to the Sultan
A Farce, acted at Steventon Jan^y: 1[7]90
spoken by Miss C[ooper] in the character of Roxalana

Lord help us! What strange foolish things are these men,
One good clever woman is fairly worth ten;
For though the vain creatures will talk by the hour,
Of woman's submission, & Man's sovereign power,
Yet we know by experience, (the best of all rules)
That the wisest of men have by us been made fools,
That howe'r for a while they may bluster and storm,

27

They will all in the end to our wishes conform.
Do you doubt? Only watch all your friends who are married,
And see by whose will household matters are carried,   10
And you'll find in all ranks, all conditions & stations,
(At least amongst polished & civilized nations)
From the Dame who in wedlock ten years has been tied,
To the Lass who has only ten months been a Bride,
That by open command, or insidious direction
My lady has got the good man in subjection.
And though to all *force* to submit he refuses,
To *oblige* her he commonly does what she chuses.
"My Dear, I'm going out – "Going out my Love! Where?"
"Only just for a walk, as the evening is fair   20
"Nay indeed you shall tell me – I must & will know"
"Why I'm going to the Club" "I declare you shan't go –
"To the club, with your cold, in such weather as this,
"I'm sure for this once you may very well miss!
"And you know the last meeting you made it so late,
"There four tedious hours at home I did wait.
"Not at home till past ten! but if men can but roam,
"They ne'er mind what their families suffer at home.
But you surely won't go" – "Why if you Ma'am refuse
Your permission, I suppose I must send an excuse".   30
"My permission! I see you have misunderstood!
I refuse! I am sure I but spoke for your good;
A Wife's my aversion her Husband who teazes,
And I beg my dear Love will do just as he pleases."
"Nay my dear! if you really – I beleive you are right,
It is as you say a most terrible night" –
Then you will stay at home to-night, won't you? – say yes,
"Ye-es-" "There, I thought so, come give me a kiss,
"You can't think dear good man how I love you for this."
Thus also – but Lord what a mad cap am I,   40
Who have tried into secrets forbidden to pry –
Who in hopes, perhaps vain, of our audience diverting,
Have dared peep behind the connubial curtain;
Yet believe me, though wildly I rattle to-night,
I am, & with reason enough in a fright.
For though I've been able by various expedients,
To reduce a proud Turk to true Christian obedience;
Though the Mufti, The Viziers, the Agas I've spurned
And an Empire's fixed laws, by a laugh overturned,

Yet vain the endeavour my fears to repress,   50
When this solemn Divan I a suppliant address,
To beg they'll accept our acknowledgments hearty,
For the honour they've done our theatrical party;
That they'll pass without censure our faults & omissions,
And try to be pleased with our light exhibitions,
That they'll cheerfully take, what was honestly meant,
Our failures forgive, & applaud our intent.

The Maid of the Moor, or the Water Fiends

On a wild Moor, all brown and bleak,
    Where broods the heath frequenting grouse,
There stood a tenement antique:
    Lord Hoppergallop's country house.
There silence reign'd with lips of glue,
    And undisturb'd maintained her law;
Save when the Owl cry'd "whoo! whoo! whoo!"
    Or the hoarse Crow croak'd "caw! caw! caw!"
Neglected mansion! – for'tis said,
    Whene'er the snow came feathering down,   10
Four barbed steeds, – from the Bull's head,
    Carried thy master up to Town.
Weak Hoppergallop! ... Lords may moan
    Who stake in London their estate,
On two small rattling bits of bone,
    On *little figure* and on *great.*
Swift whirl the wheels – He's gone – a Rose
    Remains behind, whose virgin look,
Unseen must blush in wintry snows;
    Sweet beauteous blossom! 'twas the Cook.   20
A bolder far than my weak note,
    Maid of the Moor, thy charms demand:
Eels might be proud to lose their coat,
    When skin'd by Molly Dumpling's hand.
Long had the fair one sat alone,
    Had none remain'd save only she;
She by herself had been, – if one
    Had not been left for company.

'Twas a tall youth, whose cheek's clear hue
    Was tinged with health and manly toil;   30
Cabbage he sow'd, and when it grew,
    He always cut it off to boil.
Oft would he cry "Delve, delve the hole"
    "And prune the tree, and trim the root."
"And stick the wig upon the pole"
    To scare the sparrow from the fruit."
A small mute favorite, by day,
    Follow'd his steps; – whene'er he wheels
His barrow round the garden gay,
    A bob-tail cur is at his heels.   40
Ah maul the brute creation see!
    Thy constancy oft needs the spur!
While lessons of fidelity,
    Are found in every bob-tail cur.
Hard toil'd the Youth so fresh and strong,
    While Bob-tail in his face would look,
And mark'd his master troll the song,
    "Sweet Molly Dumpling! Oh thou cook!"
For thus he sung; while Cupid smiled,
    Pleas'd that the Gard'ner own'd his dart,   50
Which prun'd his passions running wild,
    And grafted true love on his heart.
Maid of the Moor! his love return.
    True love ne'er tints the cheek with shame;
When Gard'ners hearts like hot-beds burn,
    A Cook may surely feed the flame.
Ah! not averse from love was she,
    Though pure as Heaven's snowy flake;
Both lov'd, and'though a Gard'ner he,
    He knew not what it was to rake: 60
Cold blows the blast: The night's obscure;
    The mansion's crazy wainscoats crack;
The Sun had sunk; – and all the Moor,
    Like ev'ry other Moor was black.
Alone, pale, trembling near the fire,
    The lovely Molly Dumpling sat.
Much did she fear, and much admire
    What Thomas gard'ner could be at.
List'ning, her hand supports her chin;
    But ah! no foot is heard to stir: 70

He comes not from the garden in,
    Nor he, nor little Bobtail cur.
They cannot come, sweet maid to thee!
    Flesh both of cur and man is Grass;
And what's impossible, cant be;
    And never, never comes to pass!
She paces through the Stall antique,
    To call her Thomas from his toil;
Ope's the huge door; – the hinges creak,
    Because the hinges wanted oil.   80
Thrice on the threshold of the hall,
    She "Thomas" cried with many a sob;
And thrice on Bobtail did she call,
    Exclaiming sweetly – "Bob! Bob! Bob!"
Vain Maid! a Gard'ners corpse'tis said,
    In answers can but ill succeed;
And dogs that hear when they are dead,
    Are very cunning dogs indeed!
Back through the hall she bent her way;
    All, all was solitude around!   90
The candle shed a feeble ray,
    Altho' a mole of four to th' pound.
Full closely to the fire she drew;
    Adown her cheek a salt tear stole;
When lo! – a Coffin out there flew,
    And in her apron burnt a hole.
Spiders their busy death watch tick'd;
    A certain sign that fate would frown;
The clumsy kitchen-clock, too, clicked;
    A certain sign it was not down.   100
More, and more strong her terrors rose,
    Her shadow did the maid appall;
She trembled at her lovely nose, –
    It look'd so long against the wall.
Up to her chamber damp and cold,
    She climb'd Lord Hoppergallop's stairs
Three stories high, long, dull and old –
    As great Lord's stories often are.
All Nature now appear'd to pause,
    And "o'er the one half-world, seem'd dead;"   110
No "curtain'd sleep" had she – because
    She had no curtains to her bed.

List'ning she lay;– with iron din
    The clock struck twelve, – the door flew wide,
When Thomas grimly glided in,
    With little Bobtail at his side.
Tall as the poplar, was his size;
    Green, green his waistcoat was, as leeks;
Red, red as beetroot were his eyes,
    And pale as turnips were his cheeks.   120
Soon as the Spectre she espied,
    The fear-struck damsel faintly said,
"What would my Thomas"? – he replied,
    "Oh Molly Dumpling!. I am dead."
"All in the flower of youth I fell"
    "Cut off with youth's full blossom crown'd;"
"I was not ill. but in a Well;"
    "I tumbled backwards and was drown'd."
"Four fathoms deep thy love doth lye,"
    "His faithful dog his fate doth share;"   130
"We're Fiends;– This is not he and I;"
    "We are not here, – for we are there."
"Yes two foul water-fiends are we,"
    "Maid of the Moor! attend us now;"
"Thy hour's at hand;– we come for thee."
    The little fiend-cur, cried *Bow Wow*"!
"To wind her, in her cold, cold grave,"
    "A holland sheet a maiden likes,"
"A sheet of water, thou shalt have,"
    "Such sheets there are in Holland Dykes."   140
The fiends approach.– The maid does shrink.
    Swift through the night's foul air they spin;
They took her to the green well's brink;
    And with a souse they plump'd her in.
So true the fair, so true the youth,
    Maids to this day their story tell.
And hence the Proverb rose, that Truth
    Lies in the *bottom of a Well.*

April. 1805
To Mary

1

Inconstant Month; whose varying face,
Most changeable of all the year,
Can decked with smiles to-day appear
And every soft& blooming grace;
And, ere to-morrow's sun be set,
Harsh frowns thy features may deform,
Till e'en the hardy violet
Shrinks close beneath the driving storm:
When purple clouds across the landscape sail,
And drop a mingled shower of rattling sleet & hail.   10

2

Yet, all inconstant as thou art,
With sunny morn & evening chill,
April, I will love thee still;
There's somewhat that assails the heart,
And gives a pleasure undefined,
When we behold each vernal bud
Protruding through the rugged rind,
And tint with vernal hues the wood –
When we observe the meadow's fresher green,
Marking the devious course of rivulet unseen.   20

3

Season of remembrance sweet!
Thy various works of vegetation,
Seem not so much a new creation,
As friends whom we delight to meet
After long absence of a year;
For not a vernal sight nor sound
Which strikes upon the eye or ear
Within the horizon's utmost bound,
But wakes some thought of pleasure or of pain,
And bids us live our past lives o'er again.   30

4

I love thee – for thou dost bestow
The promise sure of future good,
Which, though little understood
Haply's our greatest bliss below;
For every faint & tender tint,
Which marks, & scarcely marks the glade,
Can in the musing mind imprint
The hues of Summer's deepest shade.
Creative fancy leaps the space between,
And sees the country rich, with June's luxuriant green.   40

5

Meet emblem thou of human life;
For not with more vicissitude
Thy vernal suns & tempests rude
Maintain their elemental strife,
Than joy & pleasure, grief & pain,
The sun & tempests of the mind,
Within man's breast alternate reign;
And like thee too, in life we find
The present chiefly valued for the scope
It gives imagination wild, to picture future hope.   50

6

But yet I love thee April! most,
Because thou bring'st her natal day,
Whose influence mild & gentle sway
To feel is much my reason's boast –
Whom eight revolving years have still
Found in each trying scene of life
Anxious & earnest to fulfil
The claims of Mother, friend & wife.
Yes my loved Mary, take, nor blush to read
A Husband's well earned praise, domestic virtues meed.   60

To Edward
On the death of his first Pony – Jany. 30th: 1811

"Why weeps my boy?" his Father said;
Poor Edward points to Pony dead;
And see, with trembling voice he cries,
How stiff his limbs, how glazed his eyes;
Yes my poor humble faithful friend,
Thy life has reached its destined end.
Ne'er shall I more at early day,
Hear thy light, cheerful, welcome neigh
As to thy stall I take my way.
No more at evening or at morn,   10
Thy manger fill with sifted corn;
Fresh saintefoin put within thy rack,
Kiss thy soft cheek, or pat thy back.
No more, as in the dewy mead,
I turn thee unconfined to feed,
View thee with saucy boldness run,
John's proffered sieve & halter shun,
But quiet stand when I come near,
And let me catch thee void of fear –
No more as on thy back I ride,   20
Mark thy quick step with conscious pride,
Thy steps which scarcely print the grass,
And many a taller pony pass;
With secret pleasure view the gaze
Of travellers in the rapid chaise,
And e'er their wonder words can find,
Leave them almost a mile behind -
        These joys are flown, they come no more,
And long must I thy loss deplore;
Nor while I live, expect to see   30
A favourite I can love like thee.
Take then, my darling pony, this
My last farewell, my parting kiss."
        He spoke, & bending o'er the corse,
Kissed the last time his favourite horse;
Then slowly turned, & with a look,
Which mingled grief & love bespoke,
His Father's hand in silence took.
        That hand his Father fondly pres't,

And thus his weeping son addressed. 40
"Think not I blame your tears my love,
Pleased I behold your conduct prove
By grief so pure, so void of art,
That you possess a feeling heart.
Tis the first loss you ever knew;
A greater trial far to you
Than they can tell, who often crossed
By life's maturer ills, have lost
What nothing ever can regain,
Youth's lively sense of joy & pain. 50
Yet check awhile this burst of grief:
Let reason come to your relief. –
In every woe, at every age,
Which meets us on life's bustling stage,
The ills which we on ourselves bring,
Alone can leave a lasting sting.
Say, had you 'ere your power abused,
Had you your pony harshly used,
Had you with cruel spur & thong
Driven the poor wearied wretch along, 60
Or when oppressed with labour hard,
Left him to shiver in the yard,
Ne'er seen him littered, rubbed & fed,
How would you bear to see him dead?
How bitter then would be the thought,
You had not used him as you ought.
(But you can view, nor conscience blame,
And may you ever do the same)
Your conduct to your little steed;
For sure I am no quadraped 70
A kinder, milder master knew,
Than Pony ever found in you.
Then let this thought your bosom cheer,
Check the deep sigh, & flowing tear;
And from this loss your mind prepare,
More serious ills of life to bear. –
Happy as yet your days have flown:
More joys than sorrows you have known:
But do not think, my dearest boy,
Life is a scene of unmixed joy. 80
Your comforts always to retain,

Were hope alas! absurd & vain:
Each blessing that you now possess,
Time's lapse itself will sure make less;
And if you live, you'll live to mourn,
Full many joys that ne'er return.
Around, you now collected see
Relations, friends, & family,
Within a constant circle move,
Endeared by bonds of mutual love: 90
Yet these must all (nay do not start)
From you – & from each other part:
The time will come when every year
Takes from you some one you held dear;
Oh! then as now, may no remorse
Increase affliction's native force;
No vain regrets for joys abused,
Neglected friends & time misused,
Imprint a sorrow in your breast,
More hard to bear than all the rest,   100
May the light woes of early youth,
Teach you this salutary truth,
That every sorrow will be light,
When all within our breasts is right.
That a well regulated mind,
In each distress will Comfort find,
And unreproving Conscience, still
Provide a cure for every ill."

To Caroline – On her Birthday
June 18th: 1811

I write to please my Caroline;
No help from you fictitious Nine
I seek, nor will I beg assistance
From beings which have no existence.
Full well might such address beseem
A Heathen bard's bewildered dream,
But in my mind gives just offence
To Christianity & sense.
Affection, pious, warm & strong,

37

Alone should guide a Parent's song,   10
Inspire the thought & smoothe the verse,
That would his favourite's praise rehearse.
Yes, dearest girl, for your delight,
Improvement too, perchance, I write,
To say what plainer prose, as well
As verse, (if verse it be) can tell,
That pleased this day's return I view,
And wish as many more to you
He may grant, by whom our good
And evil, best are understood.   20
Six years my child have lapsed away,
(It seems as but the other day)
Since those blue eyes, which shine so bright,
First opened to receive the light.
And still with pleasure I recall,
Each scene that in the interval
Has marked the progress of your mind:
Proved you affectionate & kind,
Playful & light of heart, yet still
Obedient to your parents will.   30
Pleased have I seen the rising tear
At fiction's piteous tale appear,
And while I loved distinct to trace
Your Mother's features in your face,
A sweeter joy perceived, to find
Her virtues copied, in your mind.
          A promise fair of future worth;
But, as nought certain is on earth,
As all are human, all are frail,
Fear will sometimes my mind assail,   40
Lest the bright bloom of early youth,
Feeling, ingenuousness & truth,
Should shrink & vanish from the sight,
Withered by fashion's chilling blight,
And we should grieve to see our child,
By pride misled, by flattery spoiled,
Selfish, & vain, & full of art,
A modern Miss, without a heart.
But hush my fears, it will not be,
For by that sorrowing look I see,   50
(Though scarce your young & artless years

Can comprehend your Parent's fears)
You would not willingly do ought
Should give your friends one painful thought.
You would not give them cause to weep,
Or with less joy your Birth day keep.
Have I not happily expressed
The thought which swells your little breast, ⎫
And says, "indeed I'll do my best"? ⎭
    I know your resolution such,   60
But trust it not my love too much;
But pray for help to that great Power
Who gives it in temptation's hour.
That Power, who once its influence shed
On Samuel's young but pious head,
Shall hear well pleased your infant prayer,
And guide you with a Father's care,
And every year our child shall prove,
More worthy of her Parent's love.

To Miss Jane Austen the reputed Author of *Sense and Sensibility a Novel lately publish'd*

On such Subjects no Wonder that she shou'd write well,
In whom so united those qualities dwell;
Where "dear Sensibility", Sterne's darling Maid,
With Sense so attemper'd is finely pourtray'd.
Fair Elinor's Self in that Mind is exprest,
And the Feelings of Marianne live in that Breast.
Oh then, gentle Lady! continue to write,
And the Sense of your Readers t'muse & delight.
                    A Friend.

To Mary, on her Wedding Day. Jan^y: 17th: 1812

This morning was our wedding day;
And fifteen yeas have passed away,
Since fast the sacred knot was tied,
And Mary, you became my Bride.

Cold was the morn, & all around
Whitened with new fallen snow the ground.
Yet still the sun with cheering beam,
Played on the hill, & vale & stream,
And almost gave to winter's face,
Springs pleasing cheerfulness & grace.   10

A season Mary, was it not,
Prophetic of our future lot?
Emblem expressive, apt & true,
Of what I've ever found in you.
A warning fair, & kindly sent,
The hope presumptuous to prevent
That life's best joys would always last,
Nor feel affliction's wintry blast.

Yes sure, such season well pourtrays
The colour of life's chequered days.   20
In the cold rain, & snow & sleet
That'gainst the wearied traveller beat,
The whitening blast, & driving storm,
That oft the wintry sky deform
I see, methinks, in colours true,
Life's future ills exposed to view.
Life has its cold & chilling blasts;
Nor youth nor health for ever lasts;
Disease may come, with all its train
Of languor, restlessness & pain: 30
The night of feverish broken rest,
The sinking spirits, nerves oppres't,
And mortifying self denial,
The invalid's severest trial.
These I have felt, & much I fear
Must feel, while I continue here.
But yet I've comforts in my lot,
And thankless t'were to mark them not.

The sun, whose beam serene & clear,
Then lightened up the landscape drear,   40
Most aptly to my mind expres't
The sunshine of your peaceful breast.
Bade me expect in you to meet

With temper mild, & manners sweet,
With chaste affection's winning smile,
That pain & sickness can beguile
With tender & assiduous care,
My griefs to lessen or to share.
So whispered hope, nor said too much,
For I have ever found you such;   50
And often, as the newborn year
Brings back this season, cold & drear,
More welcome than the cheerful May,
Is January's wintry day.
For on that day, to me was given,
On earth, the "last, best gift of Heaven".

Then read my love, these artless lays,
And blush not at a Husband's praise,
Whom fifteen years of love, have taught
To prize your merits as he ought.   60

Lines written at Kintbury – May 1812

In this gay season, when midst genial showers
And sun's soft gleaming, spring the vernal flowers,
When each succeeding morn a brighter green
Discloses, spreading o'er the woodland scene;
'Midst scenes, whose varied landscape ever new
Presents fresh beauties to th'unsated view,
Where sloping uplands catch the sun's first beam,
Where winding through the meadow, Kennet's stream
Reflects in outline true, but tint less bright
The grey Church tower, tall tree and Mansion white;   10
Why as each well known object strikes my sight
Must pensive sorrow mix with gay delight?
Can sorrow entrance find midst scenes like these?
Can natures beauties ever cease to please?
Less softly blows the breeze or flows the stream
Than when entranced in youth's delightful dream
I mused along it's banks, nor marked the time,
How rapidly it passed, till distant chime
Of Village clock and slow retiring light

41

Proclaimed the near approach of sober night?
Ah! – No – with equal freshness blows the breeze,
And hues as vernal tint the budding trees,
Light airs as sweetly curl the rippling stream,
As softly fades the day's departing gleam.
Unchanged the scene on which so oft I've gazed;
Nor have I lost the taste (kind Heaven be praised)
To prize them as I ought; They still excite
Joys undescribed and undefined delight,
It is not that I feel their beauties less
Because I scarcely can the sigh repress; 30
Rises that sigh, because each object here
Brings back the thought of many a former year,
And faithful memory recalls the scenes
(O'erleaping the long space which intervenes)
When warm with youth and spirits light as air,
And little of life's future ills aware
The present I enjoyed and nought could see
In the perspective of Futurity
But hours of health and pleasure; ease and mirth,
A vision never realized on Earth. 40
And though life's scenes with various sorrows fraught
Have since those days a sober'r lesson taught,
I cannot yet (and if there live a man
I would not chuse him for my friend who can)
With stoic apathy and bosom cold
The scenes of youthful joys unmoved behold.
And hence the mixed sensation which I feel
Of joy and sorrow o'er my bosom steal,
Hence, while intent upon the stream I gaze
My mind reverts to scenes of other days 50
And as I trace the green and willow'd shore
I think on joys that can return no more.
　　　Yes, though full thirty years have passed away,
Fresh in my memory still appears the day
When first I trod this hospitable ground,
And welcome fair and kind reception found.
And still in my mind's eye methinks I see
The Village Pastor's chearful family.
The Father grave; yet oft with humour dry
Producing the quaint jest or shrewd reply; 60
The busy bustling Mother who like Eve

Would ever and anon the circle leave,
Her mind on hospitable thoughts intent;
Careful domestic blunders to prevent,
And ever ready on her guests to pour
The corner beaufet's rich and savoury store.
While yet a gayer group, four manly Boys
Heightened the relish of domestic joys,
Of future happiness gave promise fair
And eased with pleasing hope a Parent's care.   70
Where now are all this chearful circle flown?
Where those who once this mansion call'd their own?
Lie they at rest beneath the verdant sod
Close by the path their feet have often trod.
Not all – In distant climes, where sedgy Nile
Winds his seven streams round many a slimy Isle
One sleeps – And one where Ocean ceaseless pours
His restless waves 'gainst western India's shores;
Friend of my Soul, and Brother of my heart!
Fain would the muse in lines devoid of Art   80
Thy worth mature, and early doom relate,
Record thy virtues and deplore dry fate;
But weak is language and expression faint
The feelings true of genuine grief to paint.
For I had many a scene of pleasure plan'd
When safe return'd to thy dear native land
Thy wanderings past should a long tale afford
To friends assembled round the social board.
Much did I hope (It was a vision fair
And pity it should melt *into thin air*)   90
Our friendship soon had known a dearer tie
Than friendship self could ever yet supply,
And I had lived with confidence to join
A much loved Sister's trembling hand to thine,
So man proposes, but superior Powers
Direct the future – to submit be ours.
      Yet let me not of comforts lost complain
Unthankful for the many that remain,
Let not this spot as oft its scenes I view,
Thoughts of departed friends alone renew: 100
Well may their sight a chearful mood inspire
And teach a Husband's hand to touch the Poet's lyre.
'Twas here, in the first bloom of early youth,

All gay good humour, innocence and truth,
I saw thee Mary! and shall ne'er forget
The hour when first beneath this roof we met;
And still with fond remembrance I retrace
Each object here – and mark the very place -
The River's bank – The causeway's shaded walk
Where many an hour was passed in devious talk,   110
And every sentiment (whateer the theme)
Still raised thee higher in my heart's esteem
And soon I thought the greatest bliss on earth
To call thee mine – and know not half thy worth.
I know it now – I feel it every day –
And own with pleasure in this artless Lay   }
A debt of gratitude which nought can pay.   }

Home.
Written on returning from Kintbury – Sep^t: 1812

Through Berkshire's lanes & hedgerows green,
When, the spreading oaks between,
Peeps the landscape's varied charm,
Cornfield, mead, or sheltered farm,
Intervening copse & heath
In gay confusion, & beneath
The shelter of each sloping hill,
Many a little nameless rill
Through alders dark, or willows gray,
Or rushes, works its tangled, way;   10
Hasty through these fair scenes I passed,
And though a look approving cast
On all I saw, yet urged my way,
Nor wished to make a longer stay.
Though marked by nature's colouring warm,
It wanted one attractive charm;
Though touched by nature's master hand,
T'was not "my own, my native land".
      Hence to Highclere's varied ground,
Where in wilder form around   20
And with bolder pencil drawn,
Appear hill, valley, wood & lawn,

44

I passed, nor undelighted viewed
The hill, which steep & wild & rude,
Rising groves of oak behind
Recalls to the enquiring mind
(As high its summit trenched it rears)
The warlike chiefs of former years.
The scenery wild I much approved,
I marked, I praised, but onward moved, 30
T'was not my home – though passing fair,
My wife, my children were not there.
    Homewards still my footsteps bending,
And the sheepdown's slopes ascending,
Soon I gain the airy height,
Where no object charms the sight,
And to the eye of genuine taste,
All is but a barren waste.
Hedgerows now of verdant thorn,
The bleak enclosure's sides adorn; 40
Little verdure clothes the fields,
And the down reluctant yields
Nor healthful grass, nor verdant plant,
But russet bents, & herbage scant.
Here & there the nearer grounds,
Some copse with formal outline bounds,
And in the distance, faint & weak
Scarce appears a woody streak;
And yet this scenery, lone & rude,
With some delight I passing viewed. 50
Wild down & solitary tree,
Like good old friends appeared to me,
Who, telling that my home was near,
Gave a rough welcome, but sincere.
    These cold hills passed, more pleased I gain
The sheltered vale & woody lane,
And when the village small appears,
Scene of my early hopes & fears,
With partial fondness I declare,
No scene I've passed is half so fair. 60
For though no mountain's airy height,
With outline bold attracts the sight;
Receding gradual from the eye,
No distance melts into the sky;

Some rural beauty marks the scene,
The sloping meadow fresh & green,
The Manor house with trees surrounded,
The peasant's cot by garden bounded,
And spreading elms, beneath whose shade
My little flock secure is laid;   70
I view with joy the well known ground,
And as I turn my eyes around,
Thankful I feel that Heaven my lot
Has fixed in this delightful spot;
More thankful still when I receive
Such welcome sweet as love can give
From those, whom each revolving year,
Renders more valued & more dear –

Selbourne Hanger

"Would you view Selboume Hanger aright"
You must go when Autumn's sun shines bright,
And catches on the nearer ground;
While from th'Horizons utmost bound
Some rising clouds his brighter rays
Obscure with light and partial haze.
'Tis sweet on such a day as this,
To stand upon the precipice;
And view, at first with dazzled eye
The landscape's wild variety;   10
It's objects here in light displayed
There half concealed in neutral shade;
As misty clouds across them sail
Or vanish with the rising gale.
And when the eye with eager glance
Has ranged o'er all the wide expanse,
Survey'd the whole extent beneath;
Wander'd o'er wood and lawn and heath;
Delights it then distinct each part
To trace; and see with master art   20
How Nature works when she designs
How well each object she combines   }
Contrasts her forms, and breaks her lines. ⌡

When, with the whole combined effect
Our senses, dazzled, we collect;
The various parts we then explore –
Admire the wooded hill of Nore,
Whose steep sides give a double grace
To the low grounds that skirt it's base;
Next Frensham, note thy well known pond   30
Shine a bright speck; and far beyond
See Wolmer, whose rich scenes could claim
In former days, a Forest's name;
Now a bare waste, where bush nor tree
Breaks the dark heath's monotony.
Onward, where lessening to the sight
The hedgerows in one mass unite;
See Headly's woody vale beneath
Surrounding hills of barren heath;
And, rising to the Horizons edge   40
View Liphooks steep and broken ledge.
    Next as we trace the Zigzag walk
Cut out upon th'indented chalk,
Or rest upon the rustic seat;
Retired – yet chearful warm and neat
Midst pendant slopes of lawn and tillage
Beneath our feet appears the village.
    'Tis a sweet scene and offers much,
To tempt the Artists sketching touch;
Nor less presents a pleasing theme   50
To those who love to muse and dream
Of times and scenes long since gone by; ⎫
And to imagination's eye   ⎬
Brings back the fallen Priory.   ⎭
    Fancy recalls the distant time
When waken'd by the midnight chime
The Matin or the Vesper bell,
The holy Fathers left their cell;
And where, tall pillars massy proof
Support the chapels arched roof,   60
Chaunted the grave and solemn strain
Potent from Purgatory's pain
And the tormenting fiend's controul
To save (vain hope) the sinner's soul.
Or as they tread the cloister's walk,

Imagination hears them talk
Of saintly legends and the strict
And holy life of Benedict;
Or in less serious hour repeat
The tale of many a warlike feat   70
By wandering Pilgrim lately told ⎫
Or gallant Knight or Baron bold   ⎬
Benighted on the dreary Wold,   ⎭
And glad the Abbot's fire to share
And refectory's simple fare.
    So passed the tranquil hours of those
Who in this valley found repose,
And lost – in study or in prayer,
Each earthly joy and earthly care.
And let not these enlightened days   80
Deny some little mede of praise
To those, who thus, for what they thought
Religion – here retirement sought.
For though it cannot be denied
That Indolence and saintly Pride
And Ignorance too oft were found
Within the Priory's holy ground;
Yet numbers from the world retired,
By real Piety inspired.
Here midst the din of feudal wars   90
And civil discord's endless jars
Some gentle minds unfit to mix
In the world's bustling politics,
Or join in war's destructive rage
Studied intent the sacred page
That teaches at life's awful close
the trembling soul to find repose.
And though the truly pious mind
Can leisure and occasion find
In every scene and every place   100
The works of Providence to trace,
And midst the trifles that engage
The attention of an idle age
(While with the croud they seem to mix)
On serious thoughts their minds can fix.
Yet they ('tis sure) who love to muse
On such high themes, do mostly chuse

In pensive secrecy to dwell;
In lonely cot, or cloister'd Cell,
And in the quiet rural scene   110
Midst waving woods, or vallies green,
From the world's busy scenes apart
Delight to commune with their heart.
Deem it not fancy, for in sooth,
It is not phantasy but truth
That natures scenery lone and wild
By man unpolished and unspoiled,
The narrow valley that divides
The bold hills intersected sides,
The Forest's deep and thickening shade   120
It's ferny brakes and leaf strewn glade
Work on the mind with magic force,
And give the thoughts a purer course;
Here in reflections silent hours
The mind improves its nobler powers;
Leams to despise the Joys which flow
From sensual pleasures coarse and low;
Owns that true happiness is found
Not in the vain and giddy round
Of dissipation's endless course   130
But rises from a purer source,
From the well cultivated mind,
By learning, sense and taste refined.
By minds thus disciplined and taught,
No dangerous pleasures will be sought;
No joys high seasoned which excite
A present tumult of delight
And when their stimulus is o'er
Leave us more languid than before.
For breasts where real tastes resides   140
Nature a sober feast provides,
To calm and rational delights
Her faithful Votaries she invites.
Nature's true heirs – they seem to be
Proprietors of all they see;
More than it's Lordly owner, mark
The beauties of the rich man's park;
Oft in the foot-way-path they stop,
As pleased to see the Farmer's crop

49

Repay his skill and care and toil   150
As he whose ploughshare works the soil.
        Who talks of rational delight
When Selbourne's Hill appears in sight ⎫
And does not think of Gilbert White?   ⎬
Such sure he was – by Nature graced   ⎭
With her best gift of genuine taste;
And Providence, which cast his lot
Within this calm secluded spot,
Placed him where best the enquiring mind
Might study Nature's works, and find   160
Within her ever open book
Beauties which others overlook.
Enthusiast sweet! your vivid style
The attentive reader can beguile
Through many a page, and still excite
An Interest in whate'er you write!
For whilst observant you describe
The habits of the feathery tribe
Their Loves and Wars – their nest and Song,
We never think the tale too long.   170
With you we catch the first faint note
From the Reed-sparrows tiny throat.
Descend the Chimney's shaft to see
The twittering Swallow's progeny.
E'en the old Tortoise dull and cold
That sleeps for months beneath the mould
(Such charms your magic style imparts)
Excites an Interest in our hearts.
Oh could my rude and artless lay
Such sweet attractive charms display;   180
Could Spirit, Ease and Taste combine
To give an Interest to each line,
Ne'er would I seek fictitious theme
From fabled Wood or Hill or Stream;
Happy in loose but faithful sketch
The beauties of this scene to catch;
And Selbourne drawn with equal skill
Should live as long as Grongar Hill.

J.A. – Nov.ʳ 18:ᵗʰ 1812.

Tyger's letter to Caroline 1812

Ever honoured Mistress mine,
Condescend to read a line
Written by my little paws,
And defend poor Tyger's cause.
    Wicked Harriet has said
Tyger heavy made the bread;
Believe her not; 'tis all a lie,
Harriet spoilt the bread, not I.
Very true it is I know,
I slept a little on the dough;   10
But surely that could do no harm;
No, no, 'twas Betsey up at Farm   }
Sent her down some shocking barm
    Or else Harriet had been drinking,
Or upon her sweetheart thinking,
And did not knead the dough enough,
And when she found her bread was tough   }
Laid it on Tyger in a huff.
Tell her a shame it is that she
Should lay her careless faults on me,   20
And that I'll make her rue the day
If she again the same should say.
For, should I see a hundred mice
Eating up her tartlets nice,
I will not interrupt their fun,
I will not catch a single one.
Hence forth for me, both rat & mouse
Shall unmolested haunt the house,
Shall run about where er'e they please
And nibble bread & meat & cheese.   30
    Nay more, when Harriet goes to bed
The mice shall frisk about her head,
And when she tries her eyes to close
A rat shall bite her by the nose.
Besides, I'll tell you what I'll do,
Close at her door all night I'll mew
And such a dismal walling keep
She shall not get a wink of sleep,
Shall lose her rest, & health, & fat
Because she blamed a harmless cat.   40
    Tyger

Address to Tyger
on his stealing the steak reserved for the author's luncheo[n].

Sure you are Tyger rightly named,
A savage never to be tamed,
Of disposition wild and rude;
Yes, monster of ingratitude,
Come forth, & answer for yourself;
What made you climb upon the shelf,
And with remorseless talons take
My next day's meal, my mutton steak?
  Let all the world now judge between us;
Yes, you're a very fine Micænas,   10
Thus with fresh hunger to reward
The verses of a hungry Bard!
Who, when you slept upon the dough,
(Don't shake your tail, tis true you know)
Stood forth your champion, and took
Your part against the angry cook?
But he no more your part will take
Since this is the return you make.
What could induce you, much I wonder,
To this audacious act of plunder?   20
'Twas not by hunger you were wrought
For you are better fed than taught.
Your little mistress sees to that,
She ne'er neglects her favorite cat.
It was not mere retaliation;
I never gave you provocation;
I ne'er purloined a bit of fat
From a cold boiled or roasted rat;
And can aver with conscience clear
I have not ate a mouse this year.   30
No, 'twas an act of wanton spite,
Or else of guttling appetite.
And now I have your crime depicted,
I hope that you stand self convicted;
And will not pur a single word
Until your sentence you have heard.
  I pardon this your first offence,
And trust you have a proper sense
Of sorrow, & bewail your guilt

And mourn the gravy you have spilt.   40
But should you hence forth any more
Be caught within the pantry door,
You then to *Corbet's* shall be sent,
(Where for her crimes your sister went)
And he shall shoot you through the head,
And strip your skin off when you're dead,
And there your fur, as soft as ermine,
Shall hang midst mean & vulgar vermin;
Midst stoats & weazels shall have place,
A lesson to the tabby race;   50
That future cats may warning take
Nor dare to steal a mutton steak.

Dec^r.1812.

To Edward
On planting a lime tree on the terrace in the
meadow before the house. —January 1813

This tree which we together plant,
If Heaven a Parent's wishes grant,
For many a future year shall prove
A record of our mutual love.
While you, my boy, at school or college
Are absent, gaining useful knowledge,
Oft to this tree shall I repair,
And in my fancy meet you there;
Shall think I see your parting look,
When last a kind farewell we took;   10
And almost view the smile of joy,
Play o'er the features of my boy,
When some months hence, the wish't vacation.
From books allows him recreation,
And brings him, grown & much improved,
To Parents, home & friends beloved.
Here oft shall I delight to stray;
At the soft hour of closing day,
When the still scene & fading light,
To meditation most invite;   20

Indulge in many a pleasing dream
Of which my Edward is the theme.
Now look with pleasure on the past,
And wonder how time flew so fast,
When every morning (& what task
More pleasing can a parent ask?)
I taught my boy, whose cheerful looks
Were never damped by sight of books;
Explained some work of classic merit,
And saw him catch each Author's spirit: 30
Nor vainly tried (I think) to blend
The parent, tutor & the friend.
When every night I softly crept
Into the room where Edward slept;
(Not with more unremitting care
Did Cowper's mother once repair
To the loved chamber of her boy,
Or view him with more tender joy.)
Secured the casement close & tight,
T'exclude the chilling damps of night,   40
Then smoothed the drapery of his bed,
And on the pillow placed his head,
His night cap tied, & kissed his cheek,
Blooming with health's fresh roseate streak,
And offered up a silent prayer,
That Heaven would keep him in it's care.
Now to the future look with hope,
And give imagination scope,
With sunshine bright the view to gild,
And many an airy castle build: 50
Trust I shall live to see the day,
When I with thankful heart may say,
"Well Edward does my care repay":
See him, whate'er his lot & station,
Do credit to his education;
Shew learning's & religion's fruits
In fair & rational pursuits,
And brighten by his well earned praise,
The evening of his parent's days.
      These are my day dreams, & with you   60
It rests my boy, to prove them true;
You (with that sure & heavenly aid,

For which in vain none ever prayed)
Possess the power – oh! use it right,
To fill with calm & pure delight,
With joy unrivalled here on earth,
The hearts of those who gave you birth.
Here too I hope, when we are gone,
This place when other masters own,
When in the little spireless Fane,   70
Just seen above the woody lane,
I and your mother are at rest,
Hither, your cousin's welcome guest
You'll frequent come, & every time
Still to this interesting lime
Your visit will be duly paid;
You'll often rest beneath its shade;
Against its stem you'll often lean,
And pleased survey the well known scene.
You'll love each feature you retrace   80
Of this still interesting place:
This terrace, where you often stood,
And caught from yonder fading wood
The mellow note of distant hound,
Or the horn's hoarse but cheerful sound.
The little elm encircled mead,
Where whilome for your favourite steed
You marked a course, & on his back
Still made him keep the circling track:
The barn, where many a rainy day   90
You with your sister spent in play:
The woodwalk, where in finer weather
Beneath the shade you sat together;
All these, & every object near,
Will to your eyes more fair appear
Than any scenes you since have known:
And haply, with a sigh you'll own,
That, in life's ever varying round,
Joys pure as these you have not found.
Then too, the tender recollection   100
Of those who here with fond affection
Your childhood nurtured, & with kind
Instruction, stored your opening mind,
Will to the spot fresh interest give:

In your remembrance we shall live.
I know, & it delights me much
I know your disposition such,
That many an hour you'll linger here,
To think upon your parents dear;
On those whose care, & hope & joy,   110
Were centred in their much loved boy;
Who, whatso'ere their faults might be,
Were ever kind, I trust, to thee.

Ulysses announces to Hecuba that the Manes of Achilles demand the sacrifice of Polyxena

"Grateful I hail the morn's returning light;
"And as the sombre shades of dreary night
"Retiring fly before the Sun's first beam,
"So may each vision wild and scaring dream,
"Each superstitious terror flit away;
"And the mind brighten with the brightening day."
Thus spake, as restless from the couch she rose,
From broken slumbers, and disturbed repose,
She who was Hector's mother, Priam's wife,

Now doom'd to feel a captive's wretched life.   10
And while the line of hostile tents she view'd
Indignant thus her train of thought pursued.
"Avaunt ye visions of the midnight hour!
"O'er feebler minds exert your chilling power;
"Let Phantoms hover, and let spectres rise;
"Unreal ills can Hecuba despise:
"Long taught to feel the pang of actual woe
"I can no thought on idle dreams bestow:
"Destined, the wreck of all I loved to ,see,
"What worse can fate have in reserve for me?   20
"Widowed, and almost childless, and a slave,
"Sure I may Fortune's future malice brave:
"What untried woes can Heaven (if angry) send?
"What ills (if dreams are true) can dreams portend?
"Yet hold – of every other joy bereft,
"Have I not still one darling comfort left?

56

"Polyxena – my sole surviving child
"In person lovely, and in temper mild,
"With filial duty sooths her mothers care:–
"Yes, Hecuba is vulnerable there.   30
"But why for her encourage vain alarms?
"Her youth – her innocence – her various charms
"To Love and Pity every heart must melt,
"Others may feel what once Achilles felt.
"And I may see her, with a mothers pride,
"Some Grecian Hero's loved and honoured bride.
      Ah no; – unhappy Queen – it may not be;
Far different spousals art thou doomed to see.
With flowers indeed the sacred altar's drest,
There robed and ready stands th'expecting Priest;   40
But his affianced bride Achilles claims,
And Hymen's torch must light her funeral flames.
For see with downcast looks, and footsteps slow,
Ulysses comes to tell a tale of woe.
"Fallen Queen of Troy," he cries; while practised guile
Hides – yet scarce hides a mean malignant smile;
"I come, though most unwilling to impart
"What well may wring a wretched mother's heart;
"And much I wonder why to me was given
"A heart compassionate and soft, by Heaven?   50
"Or wherefore having such, on me impose
"The task impending sorrows to disclose?
"But thus it is: – At Aulis 'twas my lot
"(And the sad office I have ne'er forgot)
"When angry Dian vexed the wintery flood
"And claimed (atonement dire) a virgin's blood,
"Yes, 'Twas my task the dreadful truth to speak;
"Mark the pale hue of Clytemnestra's cheek;
"The power of female fortitude to prove;
"See patriot triumph o'er parental love;   60
"Plead with weak eloquence my country's cause,
"And teach her to deserve the world's applause;
"And now again: –Nay start not; –Turn not pale
"But hear with fortitude like her's the tale;   }
"Let courage in your breast like her's prevail.
"Brief let me be – upon this dreary coast
"Detained by adverse winds, our numerous host
"With eyes impatient watch each flapping sail,

"Or streamer waving with the rising gale,
"Successless watch; – no light and favouring breeze   70
"Whitens with feathery foam the ruffling seas:
"But foul and boisterous winds tempestuous sweep
"Along the surface of the blackening deep.
"The victims bleed; the due libation's poured;
"The smoking entrails by the Priests explored;
"But Heaven, till now vouchsafed not to explain
"Our guilt – And Calchas owned his art was vain.
"Last night my soldier's couch I sleeping press'd
"(When his friends suffer can Ulysses rest?)
"Thought after thought, in endless train arose,   80
"And all the long succession of our woes;
"Our dear bought victories round the Trojan wall;
"The much loved friends we saw around us fall;
"The perils we have haply yet to prove
"O'er seas which part us from the land we love;
"When Lo! – a blaze of more than mortal light
"Streamed through my tent; and seen in radiance bright
"Sudden an airy Phantom rose to view,
"And in it's form Achilles well I knew;
"A mix'd emotion in his eye was seen,   90
"Much anger, – more of sorrow marked his mien.
"Fearful I gazed, – in chilling current ran
"My curdling blood; – The spectre thus began:
"Wise Chief whose eloquence has duly won
"Those arms which erst were borne by Peleus son
"To thee – a restless shade Achilles speaks;
"Is he so soon forgotten by the Greeks?
"And can they wonder why the surges swell
"When unrevenged their once loved Hero fell?
"By treachery fell; and she yet lives whose charms   100
"Lur'd the fierce warrior from the din of arms;
"She lives, who brought him to an early tomb
"And Troy, though fallen triumphs in his doom.
"For this his angry Manes raise the storm,
"And bid wild winds the darken'd sky deform:
"And still shall favouring breezes be denied
"Till in the shades he meets his destined bride.
"Lead – to the altar lead the blooming maid,
"A victim welcome to his injured shade;
"Then hoist the sail; then work the stubborn oar,   110
"And gain in prosperous course your native shore,

Ulysses finished; – But th'unhappy Queen!
Ah who can paint her wild disordered mien?
How with the sudden stroke at first amazed
With strange and vacant look around she gazed?
How to her loved Polyxena she clung,
On every well known feature fondly hung;
And when the Priests in sad procession came
Their patient unresisting prize to claim;
Let those describe, who to describe may dare,   120
Her phrenzied look of deep and fixed despair!
Ye Christian Parents, who the parting breath
Have watched; and seen the icy hand of death
Of some loved child seal fast the closing eye,
And mark'd the last convulsive struggling sigh;
In silent anguish heard the distant knell
As sullen from the turret tolled the bell;
With many a deep drawn sigh and falling tear
Have stood around the melancholy bier;
With horror started at the unwelcome sound.   130
When the sunk coffin falling struck the ground;
And felt of rising grief a fresher gust,
While rattled on it's lid the crumbling dust;
Reluctant left the grave, with footstep slow,
And felt when home returned awakened woe
Where the small circle, and the vacant chair
Speak to your heart, your favourite is not there:
Oh think what they must feel who never knew
The comfort which Religion speaks to you?
Who in a future world no hope could see   140
Lost in the heathen wild Mythology.
Oh had they learnt what Christians since have known
No Niobe had wept herself to stone;
Nor Hecuba a life of grief and care
Had closed in hopeless comfortless despair.

Morning – to Edward

Night's shades are flown – once more the Sun
Rises, his daily course to run;
And with him rises to his toil
Who pens the Flock, or turns the Soil.
Forth come from Hamlet, Grange and Cot
The hardy race, whose destined lot
Is rural labour, and anew
Their intermitted toil pursue;
And falling copse, and furrowed field
And barn and foddered Homestall yeild   10
To the observant Traveller's, eye
A scene of chearful industry. –
Whether with slow and measured stride
The Sower steps and scatters wide
A whitening cloud of seed around
While following Harrows tear the ground;
Or if the Reaper train appear
Closing the Labours of the year,
Turn the pleased eye where'er it may
The scene around us seems to say,   20
"Man is for constant labour born,
And this and each returning morn
Bids him exert his active powers
Nor waste in sleep, life's fleeting hours,
But labour for the common weal,
And earn, e'er he receive his meal.
– Then let us rise my Edward too,
And chearfully *our* work pursue   }
For we, like them, have much to do. }
Think not nine parts of all mankind   30
Alone to labour were designed;
And that the Tenth may (as they please)
Indulge their selfish love of ease. –
No – *every* Order, Rank and Station,
Have their peculiar occupation;
And haply, there's no greater crime
Than long and wilful waste of time;-
Time the most precious boon of Heaven
To every class alike is given,

And all of their's must give account.   40
Alas! for those whose Life's amount
Contains but this, that no gross vice
Intemperance, Pride or Avarice
Have stained their lives;– if day by day
Their hours were frittered all away;
Of whom it only can be said
That they were born – and now are dead –
And all the interval between
Has been one vacant trifling scene   }
Of sluggish sloth, or pleasures mean. }   50
     Think not the idle *Poor* alone
Will live their folly to bemoan
When badly cloath'd and scantly fed
With meagre meal of parish bread
They pine their chearless hour away
In some lone hovel built with clay,
Whose shatter'd thatch and broken pane
Ill stopped with rags, admit the rain,
When with no comforts to assuage
The pains of cold, and want, and age   60
They feel and own, as sure they must
Their present state is but the just
And due reward of time mispent
Of, Sloth and Vice, the punishment.
For if their rich and high born neighours
Whose duty called for mental labours
Shrink from the duties of their state
Neglect their minds to cultivate,
If Dogs and Horses, Lines and Hooks,
(Save novels) leave no time for books,   70
They too will feel, and sore lament
The many hours of youth mispent,
And of all poverty, will find
The worst is Poverty of Mind.
– 'Twere mighty well – if youth and vigour
Would always last – to pull the trigger
Or chear the hound the live long day
And dance and flirt the night away.
But since – whatever youth may think,
The Nerves will flag, the spirits sink –   80
Unequal to the strong exertion

Of every once belov'd diversion
Since Rheumatism, Age or Gout
Will one day overtake the stout;
In life's bright morn we should provide
Against it's gloomy eventide.–
For sad in truth, is the transition
From youth to age, where no provision
In the mind's storehouse has been placed,
Where, void of talents or of taste,   90
Age, of all other joys bereft
Finds Cards the only comfort left. –
And lives, like some good folks that we know,
On honours, tricks, and great cassino –
Let such, my Boy, then be your warning,
Think it not hard to pass the morning
In turning Dictionaries over
Old Homer's meaning to discover,
To know how Grecians fought and eat,
Who pour'd the wine or cook'd the meat,   100
How pros'd the good old King of Pyle,
Or how the Lord of Ithac's Isle
Calypso's charms immortal spurned
From Circe's cup indignant turned,
And reach'd, by many a tempest tost
Thankful, his rude and rocky coast.

     Think not the labour thrown away,
The anxious toil of many a day,
To trace in Virgil's epic song
The pious Chieftain's labour long;   110
To feel the playful vein of wit
Which fills each line by Horace writ;
In Livy's circumstantial story
To view Rome's early deeds of glory;
Or mark the satire deep and keen,
When Tacitus the passing scene
Boldly describes, and paints the crimes
Which mark'd his own degenerate times.

     Though centuries away have roll'd
Since those who acted, or who told   }   120
Such deeds, within their Urns are cold   }
Though manners changed and customs new
Have given the world a different hue,

Yet in each grand & leading feature,
Unchanged will ever be man's nature,
And he, who aptly would pourtray
The manners of the passing day,
With spirit keen, & language terse,
In manly prose, or flowing verse,
And he, who learned in the laws, 130
Defends a Client's dubious cause,
In Senate leads the long debate,
And keeps attention up, though late,
Must o'er the page attentive pore,
Rich with the charms of ancient lore,
Imbibe that manly sense & spirit
Which gives a writer sterling merit;
Correct his style, & form his taste,
On classic models, pure & chaste.

They too, who would with pleasure read, 140
Of well instructed minds have need;
And great th'enjoyment we derive
To see old Authors charms revive
In many a Bard of modern day;
In our own Milton's sacred lay
See Homer's taste & spirit shine:
See Thompson's rich descriptive line,
Almost with Virgil's colouring warm,
Paint the wild horrors of the storm;
Describe the symptoms that foretel 150
Old Ocean's near approaching swell,
The wheeling sea fowls wilder scream,
The feather dancing on the stream,
The falling meteors whitening gleam.
Its' charm too, modern conversation
Owes to the force of education,
It's ancient circle dares enlarge,
Nor fears of pedantry the charge,
But rises from the beaten round
Of dress & dancing, horse & hound; 160
Discusses, with a liberal spirit,
Some modern Author's various merit;
How Scott, in simple ballad rhymes,
Records the feuds of former times;

How sense & nature still prevail
In Edgeworth's interesting tale;
Wish Southey's wild fantastic muse,
Subjects more rational would chuse;
Much praise, & slightly blame the book,
Where every pious female cook,   170
May learn, while Cœlebs they peruse,
To blend religion with ragouts.
      But most we value education,
Knowledge and taste, & information,
Because the highly cultured mind,
Resources in itself can find;
And though it does not turn aside
From light pursuits, with pedant pride,
Nor think, with gloomy superstition,
All wordly pleasure is perdition,   180
And can enjoy, with spirit hearty,
The morning's chase, the evening's party;
Yet these make not their chief enjoyments,
They are life's pleasures, not employments.
And when November's frozen sky
And snowclad hills, their sport deny,
Can with a pencil or a book
Find pleasure, nor with fretful look
And peevish murmurings, pass away,
(A plague to all their friends,) the day.   190

These are the ends, my boy, that ask
Attention to the morning's task;
For this I give my time & care,
And willingly your labour share;
Pleased and contented, when I find
Improvement in your opening mind;
Most pleased, if at some future day,
When life's gay scenes have passed away,
When spirits, health & strength are flown,
And you can dare to be alone,   200
Nor sink with shame, when you look back,
On life's long devious varied track,
Nor tremble with alarming fear,
When now it's closing scene draws near.
You then can say with honest truth,

"If free from idleness my youth,
From low puruits my manhood passed,
And, decent age is come at last;
This under Providence I owe,
To him, who in his grave lies low: 210
Yes what I am, (& let this tear,
Now falling, show my heart sincere,
I owe to you, my Father dear."

Evening
to Edward

1

The sun is now set, & the deep glowing west
Every moment fades fast to the sight,
The flocks are asleep, in their folds closely prest;
The rooks are retired to their Elm-circled nest,
And the Bat through the air wheels his flight.

2

The peasant returns, his long day's labour ended,
And sees, as his home he comes near,
From the smoke that in wide curling wreaths has ascended
And is now with the gray sober atmosphere blended
    That his fire burns chearful & clear.   10

3

Bright blazes the faggot, high bubbles the pot
And the bacon he fatted himself
In a clean earthen platter is seen smoking hot,
Nor yet is the pudding or cabbage forgot
And the brown loaf's reached down from the shelf.

4

While a dear little circle his table surround,
Does he think his day's labour was hard?
How tough was the copse wood, how stubborn the ground,
What labour it cost him to turn the flail round
    Oh! no, for he feels its' reward.   20

5

And he says to himself, this long day had I passed
    In Idleness rather than labour,
With no fire or cloathes to repell the chill blast,
Cold & hungry my cot had received me at last,
    I had fared like my indolent neighbour.

6

Had I spent at the Alehouse one half of my life,
    And in skittles & cards passed the day,
My children in rags, cross & wretched my wife,
Had rendered my cottage a sad scene of strife
    And had frightened all comfort away.   30

7

Now thanks to that Power which it's blessings so kind
On th'industrious poor man bestows.
In my family circle my comfort I find,
My prayers I can say with a true thankful mind
And contented my eyes I can close.

8

The peasant is right, & his words in good sooth
    To his betters may haply unfold
This often forgotten, but plain honest truth,
That to those who have wasted life's morning of youth
    Its' Evening is chilly & cold,   40

9.

Man is born for exertion of body & mind,
    We must all either labour or need,
And whatever our station, we surely shall find
By Providence still it is wisely designed
    That enjoyment is Industry's meed.

10

If in idle amusements our youth slipped away
    And our books lie untouched on the shelf,
Without growing wiser, our heads will grow gray
And the poor vacant mind to low spirits a prey
    Will not dare to look into itself.   50

Then let Life's early morn in exertion be passed
    In improving the mind & the heart;
And then when its' evening approaches at last,
Though we cannot but wonder its' day went so fast
    With the world we shall thankfully part;

12

Like the peasant feel glad that our day's work is o er,
Like him, hail the close of Life's Eve,
Think light of the troubles we grieved at before
Rejoice that temptation can teaze us no more
    And we soon our reward shall receive.   60

Looking back on the past, we shall think with delight,
That though faulty, we've still done our best,
Looking on to the future, shall feel no afright,
But in hope of a morning eternally bright
    Shall contentedly lie down to rest.

May 2nd. 1814

On refusing a special invitation from Mr. Chute
to meet his hounds at Mr. Villebois Cover, Chilton Wood
May 6th: 1814

1

"Why must this morn be spent in books,"?
If I interpret right his looks,
My Edward seems to say;
Why rest our horses in the stable,
To carry us completely able;
Oh! why not hunt to-day?

2

I'll tell you Boy at once, my reason;
"For all on earth there is a season";
So thought an ancient Prince,
Who had for wisdom some small credit,   10
And that with perfect truth he said it,
Experience may convince.

3

When corn is housed, & fields are clear,
And Autumn's various tints appear,
        None more enjoy than I,
To see the pack diffusely spread,
Or jostling, press to gain the head,
        With loud & cheerful cry.

4

The Farmer then no fears molest,
He rides & halloos with the rest   20
        Across his very Farm;
And if a field of new sprung wheat
Just feel the print of horses feet,
        He knows he does no harm.

5

But when, the wheat is higher grown,
And pease & oats & barley sown
And fences made up tight,
To gallop all the country over,
And cut up sainfoin, grass & clover,
Is neither fair nor right.   30

6

And small the joy, when new sown grounds,
And dry roads puzzling oft the hounds,
        All hope of sport prevent,
When violets in hedgerows growing,
And primroses in copses blowing,
        All take away the scent.

7

Besides, thus still to persevere
In hunting almost round the year,
     Has but an awkward look;
Might lead our neighbours to suspect,   40
That all improvement we neglect,
     And rarely read a book.

8

Then over bank, & hedge & ditch,
Let members great, & brewers rich,
     Bound, the fleet pack to follow;
Leading by turns the varying crash,
Let Haughty, or let Gamester dash,
     And George to Welcome halloo:

9

Let you & me, meantime my boy,
In books at home, our hours employ,   50
     And learn what we are able;
At Winton else, you'll roughly fare,
When you are placed beneath the care
     Of Doctor Henry Gabell.

10

And when at Christmas, Wykeham's rule,
Sends boys from Homer & from School,
     To ponies & mince pies,
Oh! may no frost your sport prevent,
But hazy, mild, & kind for scent,
     Be January's skies.   60

11

May you, amidst the rapid burst,
Be near enough, though not the first,
     Each leading hound to mark
And, when with eager haste they fling,
Light bounding o'er the ha ha spring,
     That fences Farleigh Park.

12

If near they meet, & fair the, weather,
We will a gallop take together,
    But do not stop for me;
The time has been, when to be last   70
I should have scorned, but that is past,
    And never more will be.

13

About the lanes I'll ride & skirt,
And sometimes be well splashed with dirt
    By half the passing field:
If quite flung out, I'll home return,
Well satisfied from you to learn
    In what a style they killed.

Lines written at Steventon in the Autumn of 1814, after refusing to exchange that Living for Marsh Gibbon in the borders of Buckinghamshire & Oxfordshire –

Ye fields & trees, amongst whose flowers & shade
Quick passed my careless childhood; scenes endeared
By many a fond remembrance; I rejoice
That duty calls me not, (as once I feared)
To bid a long adieu to all your charms;
And, like the Patriarch, to that voice divine,
Which to th'enlightened conscience clearly speaks,
Obedient, quit, not knowing where I go,
Nor what may there befall of good or ill,
My home, my kindred, & my native soil.   10
      For, though I doubt not, that had duty's call
Imperious, bid me for their sakes whom most
On earth I value, leave this dear abode,
And pitch my tent mids't strangers, I had found
The sacrifice less painful than I deemed;
Though an approving conscience, & the sense
Of having acted with no selfish views
Had lessened much my sorrow; & that time

Had reconciled my feelings to the change;
Yet much should I have suffered, when the morn   20
Arrived, on which a last & sad farewell
I must have taken to this long loved spot.
To see for the last time the morning light,
(For little sleep had visited my eyes,)
Dawn on the well known uplands, & the sun
With his pale rays obliquely slanted, tint
The tufted elm, & the low mansion's roof,
My own no longer; to have strolled once more,
(For how could I have helped it?) through the walk
Which winds, elm shaded, midst the stems antique   30
Of twisted thorn & maple; to have marked,
As through the village with unfeeling haste
The rapid carriage rattled, tree & mead
Receding from my sight, & to have lost,
As the lane's turning hid it from my view,
The last white cottage standing on the green,
A pang of sorrow to my sinking heart
Had given, felt deeply, & remembered long.
And little truly had I hoped to find
Ought in that country, where my future days   40
Seemed destined to be spent, which large amends
Might make, for what I quitted with regret.
An ampler income, & th'attendant means
Of self indulgence (to a moderate mind
And rational, at least a doubtful good,)
Were on an invalid in vain bestowed.
They cannot brace the nerve relaxed, nor give
To minds by sickness or by age unstrung,
The buoyant & elastic tone of youth.   50
        And such, (t'were vain to hide it) such is mine,
By the long habits of retired life
Unfitted to give pleasure, or be pleased
In large & noisy parties; and at times
But scarcely able to maintain my share
Of conversation, in the circle small
Of long known neighbours, & long valued friends;
How lost were I midst strangers! what were life
To me, if daily forced to mix with those
Who having never known me in those days,   60
(If ever such there were) when I had powers

Of pleasing, know me only now, as one
Who occupies a seat much better filled
By others. "What a pity this poor man
Stirs from his own fireside". – Thus sure would say
My future neighbours, and I say so too.
  Yet such society, or solitude
And sad seclusion, must have been my lot.
Alternative was none; & harder still
The lot of those, whose fate is linked to mine;   70
That little circle, whose delight or pain
I look on as my own; and dull indeed
It were for them, to spend day after day
Monotonous, unvaried by the call
Of friendly neighbours; never asked to mix
In sprightly dance, or dinner party gay.
Here they are known, & loved & valued much,
And I am known, & borne with; but who there
Would care for me or them? or what beyond
A formal morning visit once a year,   80
Done as a duty, and, as duties are,
Done most unwillingly, could we expect?
  And whatsoever fancy may suggest
Or theory may teach, there never yet
Was family so happy in itself
So centred in each other, and complete
In it's own circle, no resource to need
From social intercourse, & friendly chat
Of neighbour; & whoe'er have tried to live
Quite to themselves, & shut out all the world,   90
As troublesome intruders on their joys,
Have found at last that they presumed too much
On their own powers of pleasing, & had tasked
Their tempers & their manners, somewhat more
Than man's frail nature warrants; I have known
Those who have loved each other well, & yet
Have lived so much together, that they found
The only sure relief from sad ennui
Was mutual discord, & incessant strife.
  We are not of that number (Heaven be praised)   100
Who find domestic life a dull affair,
Unless each morning it's engagement bring:

Haply some round of visits, whose best charm
Is to find none at home; or better still,
A numerous party variously conveyed
Through dusty roads; upon barouche box high
Some mounted, & some sunk on ponies small,
To see a house, where nothing's to be seen
Except the owner's miserable taste.
We find a pencil has a powerful charm,   110
Or quiet morning's walk, to cheat the day;
We do not count the evening very dull
Unless the card table its nightly stand
Take regular, and every mental power
And faculty be quite absorbed in whist.
We love, & much enjoy with ivory knife
To sever the yet damp & clinging leaves
Of some new volume; & can pleased discuss
With critical acumen. & due skill,
An Author's merit: Authors too ourselves   120
Not seldom, & recite without much fear
To hearers kindly partial, verse or prose,
Song, parody, or tale, whose themes of high
But local import, well record the fate
Of cat or pony: or, from satire free
Raise against other's follies or our own
Perchance, the fair & inoffensive laugh.
        Yet with all these resources in our power,
Free am I to confess, the time might come
When we too should grow weary of ourselves;   130
Tire e'en of those delights we most affect,
And gladly, to diversify the scene,
Exchange our quiet for the noisy mirth
Of larger circles – find the merest chat
And gossip of the country, often deem'd
Irrational and mean, a kind relief
And needful to beguile the tedious hours
Of many a slow and lagging winter's eve.
I would not answer for myself, or those
With whom I live, that we should always keep   140
Our tempers in due order, and escape
That foe to mutual love, a habit vile
Of petty contradiction, & dissent

In trifles, did we live so much alone.
      Thus heavy might have passed the winter months
When skies inclement, and snow drifted fields
And the poached surface. of deep miry lanes
To female feet impervious, and by horse
Scarce passable, had blocked us closely in.
And when to fitful Spring's alternate scene   150
Of storm and sunshine, with reluctant step
Fair Summer months succeeded, we had found
(Or memory much deceives me) in the fields
Which skirt our future residence few charms
To tempt the lengthened walk: for though the spot
I never visited, the character and style
Of the adjacent country well I know.
For there in early days, a truant oft
From Alma Mater's discipline and rule,
In spite of imposition, or the frown   160
Of angry Dean or Tutor grave & wise,
I've dashed through boggy lane and miry field
Led by the musical and chearing notes
Of the loud echoing pack full many a mile.
– The Country grateful to the farmer's toil
I grant, and kindly to the grazier's hopes:
But to the eye of cultured taste, that dwells
On nature's sketches picturesque and wild,
'Tis unproductive, waste, and barren all.
There rich and heavy waves the wheaten crop   170
Obedient to the light autumnal breeze;
The Bean with succulent and knotted stalk
Shoots vigorous, and beneath it's broad green leaf
The whitening bloom sheds fragrance; There the Pea
Rises a perfect wood; or by it's weight
Bends downwards to the ground, from whence it sprang,
A matted heap of green and rustling haulm.
While fair beneath the cultured uplands spreads
Affording pasture to the thriving flock
And fattening herd, the green luxuriant mead.   180
But wanting is the bold and broken line
Of distant mountain; or the sloping side
Of turfy sheepwalk to diversify
The tiresome sameness of the level plain.
Of timber too there is a plenteous dearth.

No woodlands devious boundary indents
The cottage-skirted common, nor broad Oak
Spreads from the bank it's vast gigantic arms
And shades with foliage thick the road beneath.
There willows only raise their pollard heads,   190
The formal boundary of the plashy mead;
Or ozier spinny marks the winding course
Of some small nameless stream whose muddy wave
Staind with the loomy colour of its bank,
To sluggish Charwell works it's weedy way.
There too, despoiled of the luxuriant growth
Of all its lateral foliage, and the grace
Irregular and varied of its lop
The village Elm affords a meagre shade.
To such a land as this transplanted, much   200
We should have missed our native soil, and pined
Like weak Exotics just preserved alive
But faint and sickly in a foreign clime.
We should have missed the chearful morning rides
Through lanes close shaded from the noontide's beam:
We should have missed the evening walk along
The footpath leading through the varied slopes
Of airy uplands, and commanding views
Simple but chearful; Village, Farm or Grange;
Not less, but more, we should have missed the scene   210
Where in an humbler style, our small domain
Rises in gentle slopes on either side
The cottaged valley. – *Here* in varied groups
Combined, or standing single many an Elm
Uprears it's head irregular and wild,
Whose withered branches, oft projecting bare
Beyond the fringed outline of it's leaves,
To the fresh foliage grace and spirit give.
Here too the Oak, though not of largest growth,
With twisted bole and interwoven spray   220
Supports a leafy mass, whose various tint
And zig zag tracery tempts the artist's touch.
Here light of limb, and graceful in its form,
Rises the sapling Ash amidst the thorns
And brushwood of the hedge which shades it's roots.
Here too the young plantation's verdant screen
Close shelters from the cold north eastern blasts

Our house secluded; or conceals from sight
Of modern eye (more nice perhaps than wise)
The barn and homestall, which our tasteless sires   230
But prudent, placed with provident forecast
Where the inspecting eye of master keen
Might mark the tardy step of lingering swain.
Here too the Terrass from the meadows brow
Looks down upon a little quiet scene
Of simple rural beauty; sees beneath
The smoke ascend in many a curling wreath
From the low shelter'd village; or the Sun
Declining strike with rich and mellow tint
Full on the gabel end of Manor house   240
Just seen above the trees encircling shade.
Here not a peasants cottage unadorned
Is seen on either side the village road:
No ragged shed, or hovel mean disgust
The passing traveller, or make him feel
Compassion for their wretched inmates lot.
Around the poorest labourer's abode
A cultured spot sufficient for his wants
Appears, well stocked with healthy thriving crops
Of bean or colewort, or the darker green   250
And purple flower of Raleigh's valued root.
While up the cottage wall the various race
Of parasytic plants climb vigorous; and the vine
Or woodbine half obscure the little light
Of casement small just peeping from the thatch.
        These are thy charms, my native valley; these
Thy beauties; artless, but possessing much
The power of sweet attraction to my heart.
For not the eye is gratified alone
With the fair landscape; but the mind delights   260
To dwell with fond remembrance, on the thought
Of many an early pleasure, many a friend
Connected with the scene on which I gaze.
It is a feeling to the human heart
Congenial, and most potent in effect,
To long, when, absent for the welcome sight
Of the dear precincts of our native home.
The Alpine peasant hence – so legends tell,
(And I can well believe the story true)

Amidst the bustle of a soldier's life   270
Not seldom feels a longing so intense
To view the snow-clad heights, the torrents wild,
The vallies pent beneath the winding base
Of fair Helvetia's mountains; that his health
Declines apace, and mocks the healing power
Of any medicine, but his native air.
I too had haply felt, in mind at least,
Somewhat of this disease, if exiled hence.
But I am spared the trial; and I trust,
If in this changeable uncertain world   280
We can on ought depend, that what remains
Of my allotted time will here be spent,
And my Age ended where my Youth began.
– Thankful for this – more thankful still I feel
That those who share with me these quiet scenes
Are what I wish them; and the semblance fair
Of outward quiet, and repose from storms
Of angry elements, which this small spot
Exhibits;– give a picture not untrue
Of peace, and harmony, and love within.   290

J.A. July 1814.

Autumn

Let younger, gayer Poets sing
The early charms of blooming Spring
The pastured valley's fresher green
Which winds the russet heaths between;
Through the wildly wooded park
The gradual progress love to mark
Of vegetation from the hour
When spite of March's sleety shower
The furry Catkins of the willow
Blue as ocean's rising billow,   10
Or of brimstone yellower hue
Midst the coppice rise to view;
To the mild and genial day
When the latest week of May

Bids the pride of British land
Wide indented leaves expand.
Light and chearful scenes like these
Well the youthful mind may please,
Which in harmony is found
With the landscape smiling round.   20
More th'Autumnal scenes engage
Those of ripe and graver age.
The charms of each declining year
More in unison appear
With the sober turn of thought,
With the mind reluctant brought
From life's mixt scenes of joy and woe
Something of itself to know.
I love the mild autumnal light
When no more from Æther bright   30
Pours the sun his dazzling rays
But when mixt with vapoury haze
Shot in slanting lines oblique
His beams upon the distance strike.
I love to see the upland hill
Now deserted, lone and still,
Where so late the peasant croud
With acclamations long and loud
Followed in the closing train
Of the last heavy loaded wain,   40
Nor less the fading hues I love
Which tint the many colour'd grove
Where shrub and underwood and tree
In all the wild variety
Appear of Autumn's colouring drest;
Where, still distinguish'd from the rest
By many a tint of lingering green,
The Oak gives spirit to the scene:
Where the Hawthorn's rosy berry,
And ruddier leaf of wild wood cherry   50
Would, with contrast much too bright
Strike upon th'offended sight,
But that chastening hues are found
In the foliage fading round
And blackening Ash, and Birch more pale
Harmonize the woodland vale.

– Later still – when rough and rude
November's blasts assail the wood,
And at each breeze which shakes the tops
Of half stripped trees:–, incessant drops   60
A tawny shower,– and all around
With fallen leaves bestrews the ground;
E'en then I love to muse and stray
Along the glade's deep matted way;
Nor while a single leaf stays on
Think Autumn's beauties wholly gone.
Scenes like these can charm the mind
To muse and meditate inclined;
In Nature for instruction look
And draw improvement from her book.   70
For he who picturesque effects
Admires with taste, but still neglects
To draw from Nature moral hints
Is like a child, who views the Prints
In some new book with curious eye
But lets the words neglected lie.
Through the whole revolving year
Nature speaks in language clear
And in this returning season
Thus she teaches us to reason.   80
– Ended is now the round of toil
With which man cultivates the soil.
And many a month away has flown,
And many a change the earth has known,
Since first began the yearly round,
And ploughmen turned the level ground.
The field which lately waved with corn
Then by the shining share uptorn
Felt cold December's chastening frost;
In spring again transversely cross'd   90
The loose clods mouldered to the ray
Of March's sunny-windy day:
Midst April's showers the seed was sown;
In May the weeds luxuriant grown
Were by the careful weeder cleared;
In June's more genial sky appeared
The spindling stalk upright and high;
The bloom was set in hot July,

And now by August's gleam's matured
The corn is in the barn secured;   100
And, while he views full many a rick
That croud around his homestall thick,
The Farmer sees a fair reward
Nor deems his toil and labour hard.
Thus to provide the needful grain
Man's feeble body to sustain
Is a long process; and demands
The constant work of many hands;
And shall we think that less of care
Will serve provision to prepare   110
Needful for his nobler part?
Provision for his mind and heart?
– In childhood must begin the toil –
The mind of children like the soil
Parents must with anxious care
To receive the seed prepare –
– Seeds of Piety and Truth
Must be sown in early youth;
Nor must here our labour stop,
Noisome weeds of vice the crop   120
Will choak –unless with careful hand
(As weeders clear the furrow'd land)
Kindly and usefully severe
Discipline the field shall clear.
Nor seen the semblance here alone,
For most will reap what they have sown;
And when the Parent sees with Joy
As fast to manhood grows his boy,
Integrity, & worth & spirit,
United modesty & merit,   130
He deems his care & labour past,
Are amply recompensed at last.

Nor ends th'instructive lesson here;
Still the "pale declining year,"
Marked by philosophic. eyes,
Teaches us to moralize.
While on Autumn's fading hues,
And daily changing tints we muse,
Every "sear and yellow leaf"

May suggest a moral brief,   140
May lead the young to meditate,
On our own declining state;
May bid the thoughtless not presume
That youth's fresh May of early bloom
Will last for ever; but remember
That human life has its November;
That years like months, steal on apace,
And with them goes some charm or grace;
The colour fresh, the feature fair,
Th'elastic step, the lightsome air,   150
Till, like a tree of all bereft,
The human stem alone is left.
     To us, whose youth long since has flown,
The season speaks in graver tone;
Reminds us, that as woodlands pour
A thick & never ceasing shower,
So every minute tolls the bell
For man's frail race the parting knell:
So generations pass away,
And life is one autumnal day.   160
     Thus thought the Roman bard, whose strain
The scenes of Pluto's gloomy reign
Lays open fearless, & describes
The numerous late departed tribes
Of every age & rank, who mix
Assembled on the banks of Styx;
And all who read with taste, may see
The justness of his simile.
But who, that with the Poet tread
The shadowy region of the dead;   170
With him across the dull stream float,
In Charon's old and crazy boat,
Attend him to the judgment seat,
Held by the fabled King of Crete,
Elysium view, sip Lethe's stream,
And then are told, 'tis all a dream,
But must, with Christian grief deplore,
Who knew so much, should know no more.
     Then hail! Religion's purer ray,
Which leads the Christian on his way;   180

By revelation's sacred light,
He penetrates the realms of night;
Faith follows closely at his side,
Far better than the Sybil guide,
And points (where earthly pleasures cease)
To realms of happiness & peace.
  E'en in this season of the year,
When all around is dull & drear,
Amidst dark Autumn's sombre change,
His thoughts can take a wider range;   190
And while each leaf that round him falls,
Of death the serious thought recalls,
He pleased looks forward to the hour,
When like the new sprung leaf or flower
Whose root beneath the sod now lies,
The human form renewed shall rise.
Forth from their cold and watery bed
The sea shall then give up her dead;
The turfy barrows, which contain
The Chieftains fierce, in battle slain;   200
The peasant's tomb, with hazles bound,
Rising into hillocks round;
The Monarch's arched & vaulted grave,
O'er which the blazoned banners wave;
All, all shall open, & once more
Their tenants to the light restore;
In number countless as the buds,
Which burst the rind of vernal woods,
But not like them again to fear,
The blasts of the Autumnal year;   210
They dread no more the wintry tomb,
But live in Spring's eternal bloom.

The Autumn Walk
To Mary

Autumn's tints are on the trees,
Autumn's softness in the breeze;
Rising from the marshy rills
Steaming mists invest the hills;
On the sheep down's spotted side,
In many a smoky wreath divide;
And half obscure the scattered sheep
Which graze along each slopy steep;
While higher up, where morning's rays
Have wide dispersed the vapoury haze,   10
Glitter bright the turf and moss
Which clothe the summits beaconed foss.

Now's the happy favoured hour,
Ee'r winter's oft returning shower,
And frosts, the cheerless day divide,
To take the lengthened morning ride.

Then, Mary, give your fingers rest,
Lay Caroline's unfinished vest
Till Evening by, and while you may
Enjoy the last Autumnal day.   20
We'll visit every well known scene,
And trace the lanes, which broad & green
And rank with wild luxuriant grass
Give pasture to the vagrant's Ass;
Where many an ashy circle black
marks the Gipsy's bivouac.

Now the narrower copse path tread
Where wild oaks meet above our head,
And while the boughs obstruct our way
We'll push aside the leafy spray,   30
And gather from the hazel's top
The clusters ripe prepared to drop.
Emerging thence to clearer light
We'll climb some hills aspiring height
And when we gain its' verdant brow
Gaze on the woodlands stretched below,

Delighted give our eye to rove
Where hazel copse, & beechen grove
And hedgerow Elms, & oaky glade
Thicken to a mass of shade;   40
Rising o'er some woodland bower
Mark the simple village tower
In the sunbeam glitter bright,
See, beyond, the softened light
On the Landscape gradual fade;
Till lost in tint of neutral shade
Are tawny, yellow, fading green,
And (indistinct their outline seen)
Woods, fields; & copses mock the eyes
And seem to mingle with the sky.   50

Hence we'll in devious course descend
And through the lowlands homeward bend.
There the small hamlet's straggling street;
The whitened cottage tight & neat;
The old, & Elm encircled Farm
With all it's buildings snug & warm;
The leasing or the nutting group,
Who seem beneath their load to stoop,
Yet light of heart, & void of care
Their little harvest homeward bear;   60
The Farmer, who with look sedate,
Smokes, as he leans across his gate,
Counts, while they pass, his numerous flock
And joys to view his thriving stock,
Shall some what more than please the sight,
Shall give the thinking mind delight,
Shall teach our hearts to bless that hand
Which scatters plenty o'er the land,
And gives, to other lands unknown,
Joys such as Britain knows alone.   70
And when our morning stroll is done,
Warned by the low descending sun
And Evening's chill autumnal air,
We'll to our humble home repair,
Hungry, & tired enough to feel
The luxury of our simple meal;
Then round the fire, not blazing bright,

But giving an uncertain light,
About an hour we'll sit & coze
Till Evening bid the shutters close;   80
And lightened candles seem to ask
Renewal of the morning's task:
Then, while your labours you pursue,
Poem, or Novel, or Review,
With Scott, or Southey's varied Lay
Shall make the hours glide swift away;
Or if some graver work you chuse,
In sober strain th'Historic muse
Britania's triumphs shall unfold,
Her Patriots firm, & Heroes bold.   90
And while of victories past we read,
Our hearts shall glow as we proceed;
And joy to think the Minstrel's strain
Who sang their deeds might wake again
In bolder notes the song renew
And Cressy yield to Waterloo!
And when at night I close the book,
I'11 ask with a triumphant look,
If in the pale declining year
Ought very hideous there appear,   100
And try to make you fairly own,
Joy is not found in Spring alone;
But that good sense, & taste, & reason
Can pleasure find in every season;
Nay, though rough winter's blackening storm
Must soon the darkened day deform,
And the sun's disk be scarcely seen,
Pale gleaming, smoky clouds between;
Though o'er the fields December throw
His mantle cold of frozen snow,   110
And chilling skies, & Landscape drear
Their notice give of Christmas near;
Though much my comfort they annoy,
And interrupt a sportsman's joy;
And much my Sunday's ride I dread,
And I am scarcely warm in bed;
Yet will this season bring a charm
That all its' horrors may disarm;
From Venta's towers, & Itchen's stream

(Of many a youthful Bard the theme) 120
Improved in person & in mind,
The same affectionate and kind,
Eager to taste the sweets of home,
In happy hour our Boy shall come;
And when you feel his fond embrace,
And see the smile upon his face,
His happy look, his cheerful air,
Complain of winter, if you dare.

Jany 16th. 1816.

'Venta! within thy sacred fane'

Venta! within thy sacred fane
Rests many a chief, in battle slain, ·
And many a Statesman great & wise
Beneath thy hallowed pavement lies:
Tracing thy venerable pile,
Thy Gothic choir and Pillared Aisle;
Frequent we tread the vaulted grave
Where sleep the learned & the Brave.
High on the Screen on either hand
Old Saxons Monarchs Coffins stand. 10
Below beneath his sable Stone
Lies the Conquerors haughty Son;
Immured within the Chapels wall
Sleep Mitred Priest and Cardinal.
And honoured Wickham lies reclined
In Gothic tracery enshrined.

But sure since Williams purer taste
Old Walkelyn's heavier style effaced
Ore the plain roof the fret work spread
And formed the Arch with lancet head; 20
Neer did this venerable fane
More Beauty, Sense & worth contain
Than when upon a Sister's bier
Her Brothers dropt the bitter tear.

In her (rare union) were combined
A fair form and a fairer mind
Hers, Fancy quick, and clear good sense
And wit which never gave offence:
A Heart as warm as ever beat,
A Temper even calm and sweet:　　　　　　　30
Though quick and keen her mental eye
Poor natures foibles to descry
And seemed for ever on the watch
Some traits of ridicule to catch.
Yet not a word she ever pen'd
Which hurt the feelings of a friend
And not a line she ever wrote
"Which dying she would wish to blot,"
　　　But to her family alone
Her real & genuine worth was known:　　　　40
Yes! They whose lot it was to prove
Her Sisterly, her Filial love,
They saw her ready still to share
The labours of domestic care
As if their prejudice to shame;
Who jealous of fair female fame
Maintain, that literary taste
In womans mind is much displaced;
Inflames their vanity and pride,
And draws from useful work aside.　　　　　50

Such wert Thou, Sister! whilst below
In this mixt scene of joy and woe,
To have thee with us it was given
A special kind behest of Heaven.
What now thou art! we cannot tell:
Now where, the just made perfect dwell
Know we as yet: to us denied
To draw that parting veil aside,
Which twixt two different worlds outspread
Divides the Living from the Dead.　　　　　60
But yet with all humility,
The change, we trust was fair for thee.
For oh! If so much genuine worth
In its imperfect state on earth

So fair and so attractive proved
By all around admired and loved:
Who then the Change dare calculate
Attendant on that happy state,
When by the body unconfined
All Sense, Intelligence and mind   70
By Seraphs born through realms of light
(While Angles gladden at the sight)
The Atherial Spirit wings its way
To regions of attendant day. –

Lines written in the Autumn of 1817
after a recovery from sickness.

Gay Summer's sunny noons & evenings mild
Are over; soon they passed, & Autumn now
Comes on apace, & brings the shortening day,
The morning misty, & the evening chill.
Fields change with changing skies; the cultured plain
Displays no more a verdant wood of corn,
Waving its high tops to the rustling breeze,
But shows a varied surface; wholly cleared
Here by the farmer's hand; there spotted still
With many a tufted heap, decreasing fast   10
As the wain passes on from row to row,
Its size augmenting while it moves along.
Still farther on, in many a little patch
Of form irregular, the bending stalks
Of ripened barley, fall beneath the stroke
Of stooping mowers, whose progressive course,
The new sprung trefoil marks with fresher green.
Beyond, the blackening leaves of standing beans
Or seeded clover, mix their chastening tint
And harmonize the whole. Nor wanting yet   20
A group of humble leasers, wide dispersed
O'er many a stubble; or returning home,
Their heads low bending with the well piled heap.
The sun meanwhile, through fleecy bright edged clouds

Sheds a mild radiance, & throws softer light
O'er all the landscape. 'Tis a pleasing scene,
But evanescent. & succeeded soon
By one less cheerful; Leaves, fast falling round,
And half stripped groves, & uplands spreading wide
A black extent of withered russet lawns,   30
Or dun discoloured stubbles; & below
Lone meadows floated by the ceaseless showers
Which swell the small stream of some nameless brook,
And bid the muddy tinctured rill o'erflow,
Impatient of restraint, its winding banks.
Sad change to most; for few can see a charm
In nature's fairest scenes, unless adorned
With Spring's fresh green or Summer's foliage rich.
But not to me delightless is the sight
Of fields & trees, while yet the faintest streak   40
Of lingering green, releives the russet hue
Of the small sheltered meadow; while the beech
Or stunted oak, which clothes the steep hill's side,
Retain a mass of russet coloured leaves –
I love to wander through the rustling glades
Of the tall beechen grove; or trace my way
Through the long narrow path, which winds along
Amidst the overhanging underwood; or climbs
The heathy slope, with brushwood intermixed,
When all around is still, nor sound is heard   50
To break the solemn silence; save perchance
Some solitary red-breast cheers the scene,
With sweet but feeble note. A season this
Which fits the mind for contemplation deep,
And tempts to many a pleasing reverie
Of castle building thought. – I loved such scenes,
E'en in the flush & hey day of my youth,
In life's fresh spring; far more appropriate now,
For I am in the Autumn of my days,
And must prepare for winter. – Sickness too,   60
And sorrow have of late with force combined
Assailed both mind & body, & disposed,
(Whom will they not dispose?) to sober thought
Arid serious meditation; & with these
The faded tints, grey mists & hazy skies,
Which mark th'Autumnal season's parting hours,

Are much in unison; they well pourtray
The change which waits upon declining life –
For who can view the bare & naked boughs,
Rough stems, & leafless spray of yon tall trees,   70
So late with summer's foliage rich & gay,
Nor think on the frail state of mortal man?
Nor feel reminded of that change more great,
Which time is hourly working in ourselves?
How every year in its progressive course
Steals something which adorned the human form:
Silent but irresistible, bears off
Youth's grace & bloom, & manhood's strength of limb,
And leaves a naked, withered trunk alone,
Resembling much the wintry forest's stems.   80
The leafy mass we tread beneath our feet,
Covering the foliage of each former year
In many a separate layer, may bid us think
How fast man's generations pass away;
Remind us of our last abode on earth,
The church-yard, & the grave, where rest the dead
Of many a century; where sculls & bones
And mouldered coffins, by the sexton's spade
Upturned, must yield a place to those who died
But yesterday; themselves to be displaced   90
In turn, by those who drop in future years.
        Nature, in every season, is a book
Open, for man's instruction, & no leaf
Is more improving than th'autumnal months.
O! let me not neglect the moral page
Unmarked, or read it with a careless eye,,
Or turn disgusted with the keen reproof
Which haply it may give, or deem the kind
And salutary lesson, but a harsh
And needless interruption to my joys;   100
But note attentive every various hint,
And treasure up the warning, which Heav'n sends
In this, or any form; for varying oft
And manifold, the means which Heaven provides
To bring us to our senses, & a due
Sobriety of mind; else surely lost
Amidst the noise, & bustle & turmoil
Of worldly occupations; most of all,

When with rebukes God chastens man for sin,
And sickness, like the all devouring moth,   110
Corrodes the garments of our mortal frame.
      Yes, there is nothing like the sick man's bed,
To teach the sufferer wisdom; for with health,
High thoughts & pride of heart at once take flight;
We feel what poor dependant things we are,
How little we can do to help ourselves
When danger threatens; e'en if danger none
Should threaten life; confinement close & long
Seclusion from the air, & cheerful face
Of nature, & the gay & social meal   120
And friendly intercourse with those we love,
May well abate the buoyant spirit light;,
And thoughtlessness of mind, which oft attends
Uninterrupted health, & hours of ease.
The tedious sameness of the long, long day,
Unvaried, save by the physician's call;
The night more tedious, when hour after hour
We count the striking clock, & seem to think
The day will never come, give ample room
And very meet occasion, "with our hearts   130
To commune in our chambers, & be still".
Oh! who can then forbear to turn a thought
On his past days? Or who without regret
Can take a retrospective view of life?
Where now the vain, deceitful argument,
The fond delusion, apt & plausible,
Which hushed that troublesome, intrusive foe,
Our conscience; which spake peace when there was none,
And reconciled the sinner to himself?
In what an altered form does many a deed,   140
And many a word, & many a thought appear,
Cleansed from the obscuring haze, which worldly love
(Like fogs autumnal on the distant hill)
Round every object threw; distinctly seen,
Since reason, like the sun's meridian disk
Emerging, dissipates the vapoury cloud,
In their true shape & colour! – Seems it now,
(It did so lately,) but a light offence
To waste our time, for nobler ends bestowed,
In vain & trifling pleasures; in pursuits   150

But barely innocent of actual guilt;
At best irrational, & mean & low,
At war with all improvement of the mind,
And incompatible with serious thought,
Or useful occupation? Was it well,
That with unfeeling carelessness, we spent
In selfish luxury, all our worldly goods,
Wilfully ignorant how many pined
In sickness & in want? and if perchance
Some casual fit of feeling, or the sight   160
Of actual misery, moved us to bestow
A trifling dole of charity, scarce missed
From our superfluous wealth, we fondly deemed
That duty asked no more, & claimed a right
To give to self indulgence all the rest;
Say, shall we then presume to call each fit
Of transient seriousness, each feeble wish,
Each half formed resolution, (soon broke through)
Of an amended life, by the mocked name
Of penitence? Or think a few good deeds,   170
So thinly sown through many a wasted year
Of idleness, will save us from the charge
Of having hid our talent; buried deep
The pound committed to our special care?
These, & unnumbered most alarming thoughts
Will, though unbidden & unwelcome, rise,
Not easily dismissed. The magic spell
Which blinding long our not unwilling eyes,
Deceived us, (for we loved to be deceived)
Will then be broken; the bewitching draught   180
Of the Circean cup, will then have lost
It's potency; and our awakened minds
Regain at once their long suspended force,
Nor longer mocked by strange fantastic forms,
Will view all objects in their real shape.
Oh! what a strange, confused & wildered dream
Will life's past scenes, at such an hour appear!
How vain & unsubstantial all its joys!
How little worth the toil & anxious thought
And earnest care with which we still pursued them.   190
How oft we set our hearts, & built our hopes
Of lasting happiness, on some event,

92

Which when it came, came only to elude
And mock & disappoint our air built schemes.
How pertinaciously we still adhered,
(In spite of past experience) to the fond
Long cherished expectation, that the years
To come will give us what the past denied,
What they must fail to give, (earth has it not)
Unmixed delight, & pleasure unalloyed.   200

   Thrice happy they, & happy they alone,
Whose retrospective view of life's past scenes
Is cheerful & consoling; & presents
But little to regret for time misspent,
And not unhappy, whom Heaven's chastening hand
Corrects, but not in anger, & awakes
By sickness, to such train of serious thought,
And such a just conception of themselves,
As well befits man's frail & erring state;
Who wisely take the warning kindly sent,   210
And thankful from the couch of sickness rise,
At once to bodily & mental health.

   Be this my lot, (for with the first, myself
To count, I dare not; yes, be this my lot;
And often as the quick revolving year
Brings back th'autumnal season's varied tints,
Oh! may it still bring back remembrance fresh
Of danger past, of sufferings undergone.
Recall the feelings, all the fears & hopes
Of an awakened mind; and give new force   220
To slack & faltering resolution – "whet
My almost blunted purpose", & secure
My heart from imperceptible relapse
To worldly vanities, so oft abjured.
Oh! may my future years, (if years are given)
Be passed in profitable studies, such
As fit the serious & reflecting mind
For due discharge of that important trust
Committed to my care. Be this my first
My daily occupation; this employ   230
The early hour of morning, when the mind
Is fresh & vigorous from the night's repose,
Calm & unruffled yet by earthly cares,
And all the intrusive business of the day.

93

Be this my life's grand object; the great end
Of all my serious studies & pursuits.
And for those hours which relaxation need,
And lighter occupation, may I find
An innocent resource in such alone
As reason warrants, & good taste approves.   240
For even by our pleasures, & the way
In which we spend our vacant hours, are marked
The characters & features of our mind.
Oft have I thought, & much I love to think,
That Providence, with gracious kind intent
To make our trial easier, gives us all
A taste for some unblameable pursuit,
Which saves us from temptation, & the bane
Of dissipation's coarse & sensual joys.
        To analyze, transmute & reproduce   250
With chemic science, the component parts
Of earth, air, water, & to ascertain
By fresh experiments, the latent powers
Of the metallic produce of the mine,
To some affords a never failing source
Of innocent delight. – From the green bank
Which bounds the narrow lane, so thick besprent
With flowrets wild, & herbs, & spicy grass,
Another finds amusement; pleased to cull
His green & various harvest, & arrange   260
With skill Linnean, every plant distinct
In its due class & order. Most of all
The farm, the garden & the green house yield
A pleasing occupation, & refresh
By welcome, salutary interchange
Of lighter cares, the mind & spirits pressed
With serious business, or with study deep.
Such would I choose; & grateful let me feel
That Providence has placed me in a state
Most friendly to my wishes; that my home   270
Enjoys (however little else it boasts)
The charm of rural quiet; far removed
From the thronged city's bustle, smoke & noise,
And ever passing crowd. I would not change
For the gay Theatre's high coloured scenes,
The chaster hues of nature; or give up

E'en for those glowing tints which Glover's hand
Spreads on the mimic landscape, (though I gaze
With high delight upon his magic touch)
The real streaks of morning's opening light,   280
Or richer hue of evening's saffron sky.
Th'assembled party, where a well dressed mob
Elbow each other, to the vast delight
Of the large mansion's mistress, pleased to see
So many made uneasy at her call,
Holds out no charms for me; far more amused
To plant the sapling; nurse & tend with care
The rising tree; to clear away the fence
Which with an awkward line divides my fields,
Or lead the narrow walk through hedgerow wild   290
With broad leaved hazle shaded; & improve
As best I may, my quiet small domain.
Who finds an interest in pursuits like these
And harmless occupation, little fears
The change of seasons; sure of a resource
In winter's gloomiest hours. – But most I prize
And cultivate that taste for nature's charms
Which teaches me to view her simplest scenes
With high & indescribable delight.
This makes me Lord of all I see around;   300
My neighbour's lawns, & fields, & woods are mine;
Mine, by the title deeds of genuine taste,
And I enjoy their produce; pleased to see
The country fast improving, view the fields
So lately marked with many a formal line
By the plough's steady course, & half the year
A brown extent of fallow, verdant now
With turf & foliage fresh, & sprinkled well
With sheep & kine, which graze beneath the shade
Of many a young plantation's thriving trees.   310
And though 'tis true that nature's wilder scenes,
Which mock th'improvements of man's puny hand,
Delight me more; the forest & the lake,
The cloud topp'd mountain, & the cliff abrupt
Washed by the flashing surge, & yeasty wave,
Yet are those tamer features pleasing still,
Which mark the inland landscape's quiet scene.
True taste is not fastidious, nor rejects,

Although they may not come within the rule
Of composition pure & picturesque,   320
Unnumbered simple scenes, which fill the leaves
Of nature's sketchbook; but delighted, dwells,
E'en where a whole is wanting, on some part
Of fore or distant ground, which well may tempt
The pencils spirited & vigorous touch.
The manor house, converted to a farm,
Whose pointed gable, & stacked chimneys rise
Above co-eval sycamore & elm
The cawing rooks abode. The cottage lone
With insulated garden, & small close   330
Stolen from the heathy waste; the sheltered lane
Shaded on either side by spreading oaks
The small contracted vale of fresher green
That sinuous winds in devious course beneath
The tufted sheepdowns steep ascending slopes.
These, (& no district of Britannia's land
Boasts not such simple scenery) charms possess
Attractive to the eye of cultured taste.
They give delight to many a morning's ride
And many a moonlight evening's quiet walk.   340
To pause & meditate on scenes like these
May not unaptly fill a vacant hour,
So spent, not wasted; hence we often draw
Some moral lesson or improving hint,
And while we please the eye, inform the mind.
          The various produce of the cultured soil,
Its waving harvests, & its flocks & herds
Which grace the clovered vale, or spreading crop
The level lawn, or thymy mountain's brow,
Bespeak the kindly hand of Providence   350
Working unseen, (or seen in its effects
Alone,) for man, & all his num'rous wants,
And tempering with such nice & constant care
Each season's changes, such proportion due
Allotting, (whatsoever some may deem)
Of rain & sunshine, as may best promote
The work of vegetation; fill the floor
With winnowed grain, & to the healthy flock
Prolific, give its annual large encrease.

Who says that miracles have ceased? The world   360
Is full of wonders; every year displays
The miracle of harvest; and that hand
Which erst in Sinai's wilderness rained down
The pearly manna, or compelled the winds
To waft the numerous quails to Israel's camp,
Still kindly provident, supplies our food
By causes equally to us unknown.
Wake not these scenes such thoughts within our breasts,
We are most dull indeed; & worse than dull,
If we can feel them, & be thankless still.   370
    Let not such guilt be ever mine; nor taste
That bids me mark with exquisite delight
Fair nature's scenery, & in nothing more
Than a mere harmless, innocent resource
To fill an idle hour; but dare to claim
A more important office, & become
Religion's handmaid; elevate my mind
Above this little quickly changing scene;
Give me to view the world in its true light,
Nor prize beyond their real & genuine worth   380
Its purest & most rational delights;
Nor, heedless with what haste they glide away,
Year after year unprofitably waste
In idle pleasures, or low thoughted cares;
And, wondering much that they have flown so soon,
In spite of many a warning, be surprised
By sudden death at threescore years & ten,
Oft as I see, (& sweet it is to mark)
The various seasons of the circling year,
And note with what a still & silent course   390
They slide into each other, how the blasts
Of winter, oft returning gradual yield
To the mild breezes of the genial Spring;
How imperceptibly the tender hues
Of new sprung leaves, assumes the deeper dye
Of summer's richest foliage; or how soon
The watchful eye attentive may detect
The lurking yellow, brown & ochery tints
Of Autumn stealing on; itself to change
As silently to winter's gloomy skies,   400

Or snow's monotonous & dazzling white.
Oh! may I well reflect that human life
Is here pourtrayed; that like the passing year
By changes imperceptible but sure
Our infancy, youth, manhood & old age
Pass their respective bounds, succeeding each
In such a silent progress, as escapes
The notice of a light & careless mind.
  E'en while I write this desultory strain,
How changed is all around me! Autumn saw   410
My little task commence; her pencil then
Had lightly touched the early withering leaves
Of lime & chesnut, while the village elms,
Which screen the cottage garden from the road,
Showed but a duller green, & fresher still
The woodland oak retained it's summer hue.
The sun too threw a sweet & parting beam,
With just sufficient warmth to clear away
The morning fogs, which floated on the side
Of many a hazy hill & open fair   420
The varied beauties of the vale below.
But these, & every mild Autumnal charm
Are vanished now; & scarce a faded leaf
Hangs on the oak's bare branches; scarce a gleam,
Shot from the sun's pale disk, midst parting clouds,
Appears to cheer the dreary winter's day.
Loud howl the hollow winds, or ceaseless showers
Pour down in torrents; Trees but ill defend
The venturous walker, who pursues his way
Beneath the forest's ever dripping boughs.   430
Around all cold & cheerless; from within
Our best & fairest pleasures now must rise;
Nor are they few, or difficult to find.
Cheerful the blazing fire, more cheerful still
The converse & society of friends
Collected round; each willing to produce
From memory's treasured store, what best may give
Amusement or instruction to the rest;
Tale, anecdote, or incident long passed,
Or the light news & gossip of the day,   440
If told with spirit, then have each their charm.

Flags conversation? Quite exhausted all
The subjects which our quiet life affords?
Books are a sure resource; the poet's lay,
Th'Historian's record, or the Traveller's route,
Or fiction's lighter tale shall lend their aid
To cheat December's evening of its length.
Nay more perchance, (& I am well repaid
If so it prove,), these rude & artless lines,
A sketch of my mind's feeling, & composed   450
To pass a vacant hour, else worse employed,
May do the same kind office; and may find
Collected round the blazing Christmas fire
An audience, who, by partial kindness led,
May deem them poetry, & smile applause.

The Œconomy of Rural Life

The following Poem was begun in the Summer of 1819, and
was left unfinished a few weeks before the Writer's death.

Of rural life the enjoyments & the cares,
The pleasure & the duties, (for on these
Performed with pure sincerity of heart,
Enjoyment worth the name alone attends)
I sing adventurous; yet I fain would think
Not rashly daring or unqualified
For such a pleasing task. From earliest youth
To now declining years, my days have passed
Far from the smoke & din of Towns:
"And little of this great world can I speak   10
Save what pertains" to rural walks & shades,
Spring's green approach, & Autumn's fading close.
The seasons & the scenery around
Have been my best instructors; I have loved
To muse & meditate, & moral hints
From nature's ever varying scenes to draw;
Delighted most when I have thought I found
"Tongues in the trees, books in the running brooks,
Sermons in stones, & good in every thing."

Who does not love the country? or at least   20
Who does not feel delight in rural scenes
At certain seasons? 'Tis a taste innate
In almost every mind, & though suppressed
By occupation, habits & abode
Averse to its indulgence, rarely quite
Extinguished, but will ever & anon
Appear, where least expected to be seen.
Hence the delight the city's inmate takes
In glass conspicuous on the chimney placed
To rear the early hyacinth, & deck   30
With myrtle or geranium's fragrant leaf
Balcony or veranda – or if slender means
Forbid to purchase the gay painted vase,
They plant in brown glazed pot, or fractured bowl
.Their tiny garden, or the dead blank wall
Which bounds their small paved court, where never yet
Intruded sunbeam; clothe with creeper light
Whose leaf is rather any tint than green.
Hence they who toil in dusky office pent,
For six long days; upon the seventh emerge,   40
And take their weekly portion of fresh air
With double relish. – Every thing around
Delights them; & though haply never taught
By Gilpin or by Price to judge by rule;
To praise, where praise is due, & regulate
Their admiration by the Canon law
Of orthodox & genuine taste; they find
Sufficient to admire in all they see.
For them the nursery grounds & garden trim,
The field half rural, where in little space   50
Corn, grass & fruit trees all are interspersed
In whimsical confusion, are beheld
With highest approbation & delight.
Perhaps they envy too his happier lot,
Whom prosperous commerce, & increasing wealth
Have made the Master of some Villa small
Hard by the dusty road: well pleased they view
Peeping between the stumps of poplar tall
And guarded by Chinese or Gothic pale,
His sweep diminutive, his close cut hedge,   60
And garden of two perches & a half.

The country much they praise, & much they long
Impatient for the day when competence
Shall free them from the counter & the desk,
And place them snug within some rural box
Which they may call their own. – Most true it is
That should they live to realise this dream
Of future comfort, they may chance to find
(As castle builders oft have found before)
Enjoyment will not pay the claims of hope.   70
Yet argue not from hence, the general love
Of rural scenery, & a country life
Is all delusion; think rather they require
Some previous disposition of the mind,
Some well formed habits; & who has them not,
Settle where'ere he may, in hamlet small,
Lone house, or village populous, will find
That he is little gainer by the change.
Hence comes it, that not all whose earliest youth
Was nurtured in the country, love it yet,   80
(What'ere they fancy, for itself alone.
They prize it for some pleasure which it brings
Congenial to their habits & their taste.
Thus when they praise a rural life, some mean
The horse, the hound, the fowling piece & rod.
The trees must drop their leaves, ere they can find
Charms in the forest glade; & stubbles bare
And faded meadows rank with grass & weeds
Autumnal, must usurp & fill the place
Of waving pastures, & of pastures green,   90
Ere they enjoy the prospect; and the brook
Blacken with curling winds; its once clear wave
Run muddy stained with rain, & help deceive
Its scaly inmates, ere its winding banks
Attract their footsteps. – Take away these charms,
And they would quit the fairest spot on earth,
Leave cheerful sunshine, pure cerulean skies,
Air healthful & elastic, for the gross
And smoky atmosphere – the dustiest street
Of the most dusty Town; where pent up crowds   100
Miscalled society, with mutual zeal
Kindly prevent intrusive thought, & keep
The mind in happy ignorance of itself.

101

Call we for proof? In Springs returning months
When from the blooming shrubbery the breeze
Blows balmy; & dispenses all around
The grateful scent of the expanding flower;
What time the larch its fresh & tender green
Puts forth; when primrose & anemone
Upspringing quick conceal the matted leaves,   110
The winter carpet of the hedgerow glen,
With rich & varied tint of flower & leaf;
Where is the Lord & Owner of these scenes?
Strolls he with tasteful joy his lawn around,
His garden or his park? – Oh no! – far hence
He flies, regardless of their beauties – found
At Theatre or Ball, amidst the crowd
Of Britain's thronged metropolis; for know
A London winter now begins in May.
His favourite sports protracted, till the fence   120
New made, forbids intrusion on the field:
Till bladed wheat, & beans expanding leaf
Cry shame upon his courser's murderous track;
He quits reluctant; but that effort o'er,
With no reluctance quits his fair domain,
Till Autumn shall renew its power to charm.
How true we find, that rural life requires
The mind to have resources in itself;
For in the City's almost endless scenes
Of light amusement, Opera, & Rout,   130
And Exhibition, minds of little power
May find a something which in part conceals
E'en from themselves, their mental penury,
That leanness of the soul, which dwells within.
But these, the Country knows not; once a month
At most, returns the Club; & moonless nights
And hollow roads filled up by snow, forbid
The social dinner – Coffee house is none;
Gas lighted street, gay shop, or rich Bazaar,
No gape seed for the eye; & for the ear   140
No gossip; save the uninteresting tale
Of village scandal; or prophetic threat
Of crops destroyed by wire worm, frost or blight.

And can we ask for rational pursuits,
For occupations innocent & pure,
Employments useful, which at once combine,
Deemed falsely inconsistent, by the crowd
Of fashion's votaries, duty & delight.
Was all once taught at College & at School
Taught for no better purpose, than to keep 150
From truant idleness, or worse pursuits
Th'unsteady years of boyhood or of youth?
Or that at best the trembling candidate
For Academic honors, well may pass
The fiery ordeal of the public schools,
And that dread trial over, read no more?
If haply no professional pursuit
Makes study needful as the price of bread.
If love of knowledge, & a fair desire
For rational improvement, with the gown 160
Are to be left behind – but ill bestowed
The three years labour of the studious youth.
Imports it little to have gained a stock
Of sterling classic lore – or formed the taste
On Grecian or on Roman models pure;
To have improved the mental powers by all
That Euclid or the Stagyrite can teach,
If trifling.pleasures, & pursuits at best
Irrational, are henceforth to debase
The nobler powers, & blunt the faculties, 170
And vitiate the taste – till he, who once
Seemed formed for something better; whose first years,
And young attainments yielded promise fair
(And 'tis the lot of numbers,) loses now
All relish for the pleasures of the mind;
Sensual; & self indulgent, rude & coarse,
Into the Sportsman or the Farmer sinks.
Avoid such wilful degradation, ye
Whom early independance, much the wish,
Still more the bane of gay & thoughtless youth 180
Exposes to Temptation. – Oh! restrain,
Betimes restrain the enervating attack
Of indolence, with whose bewitching spell
Compared, Circean cup were innocent & safe.
Let not your volumes on their quiet shelf

Grow rusty from disuse – or moved alone
When cloud incessant rising after cloud
Pours down cold showers upon the plashy ground.
Not that I deem it needful to turn o'er
The glossary, or grammar's heavy leaf,   190
Or to unravel with the patient toil
Of German Scoliast, the page perplext
Of a dead language. – In our native tongue
Composed, but with true classic taste expres't,
Unnumber'd works of genius & of taste,
Historic or didactic, records old,
Or tales of other times, rehearsing deeds
Heroic, or more valuable still,
The well enlightened Spirit of our Sires,
Who framed Britannia's fair impartial laws,   200
Solicit your attention, & will pay
With ample interest every hour you give
From idle pleasures taken, to pour o'er
Their mind enlightening & instructive page.
Thence shall you best that general knowledge gain
Which well befits the station you are called
To fill – An English Country Gentleman.
Not scientifically deep, nor yet
Professional alone; but such as gives
Expansion to the thought; a wider range   210
To mental powers, & much exalts the taste
Above the narrowly contracted views,
The little round of mean *low thoughted cares*,
Which ever occupy unlettered minds.

Who reads the page of Clarendon or Hume,
And is not thankful that he lives in days
When Britain's well poised constitution gives
Security to all? Who shuts the book,
Nor feels a love for Liberty, combined
With Loyalty, warn, rational & pure?   220
Much needed now, to check the intemperate zeal
Of mimic Patriots, & Reformers wild,
And to transmit uninjured to our sons,
Our laws, our liberties, & chartered rights.
Nor is this all – though this might well suffice
To justify & recompense the hours

To books devoted – For they little know
To estimate the influence & extent
Of mental culture, who confine its use
To deep & serious subjects – not aware   230
How many a source of innocent delight
And interesting pleasure they forego,
Who pass their days in shapeless idleness;
Who live in ignorance profound & deep
Of all but animal & sensual joys.

    Astronomy, (nay start not at the sound,
It is not needful to be deeply learn'd
In Newton or Copernicus) will add
Charms to the evening walk, when Autumn's skies
Are bright with harvest moons, & rising fair   240
Amidst the twilight of the darkening west,
Arcturus leads the long succeeding train
Of twinkling stars, which take their station fix'd
On the arched cope of Heaven; or shining fair
With steady light, the wandering planets trace
Their desultory path. To know their names
And distances, the hours at which they rise
Or sink again beneath th'horizon's edge,
Their motion, to the uninstructed eye confused
Apparently, but with true wisdom framed,   250
Impelled & guided in their devious track
By laws not to be broken – raises much
The pleasure which their shining lustre gives;
Excites a noble interest in the mind,
Which thoughtless ignorance can never feel.
Does the gay border, edged with various plants,
Or woodland bank with wilder verdure crowned,
And self sprung flowrets, more attract your taste?
A slight acquaintance with botanic skill
Will much increase the pleasure you receive   260
From vernal walks; & teach you how to class
And to distinguish, not indeed
Like Judah's king, all vegetable life;
From cedar down to hyssop, but enough
Of skill, to mark the common herbs & plants,
Which your own fields produce; to know
Their leaf, their colour, property & use. –

But does thy mind require a wider range?
Accompany the venturous traveller
To distant lands; their climates, & their soils,   270
Their various habits & their manners note.
One profitable lesson may at least
Be learned by all; to cherish for their native land
More natural affection; nor complain
That fogs & mists so oft obscure our skies;
That winter more than its due share usurps,
And lingers long, & oft returning still,
Deforms the beauty of the vernal months,
While we are free from far more serious ills,
Which other climates feel. No summer suns   280
Inflame the feverish blood, & bring disease
And death – No rainy season here
 Week after week confines us to the house;
But weather temperate though changeable
Allows for wholesome exercise & air,
Some day in every season of the year,
Some hour of almost every passing day.

        Nor would I from my list of books, exclude
With taste fastidious & affected, works
Of fiction – tale, or novel or romance,   290
Which most who read, ungratefully deny.
Who can the Highland cave of Donald tread,
Without a fearful feeling of delight?
Who, Waverley's enthusiastic mind,
Misguided as it was, can wholly blame?
Who feels not a sensation undefined
Of awe inspiring pleasure, at the hut
Of Elspeth? And her tale, now lost, & now
Resumed again, as reason ebbed & flowed? –
Who does not love the pure simplicity   300
And heart affectionate of Jeanie Deans,
Or tremble anxious for poor Effie's fate?

        With such resources, dare you to complain
Shameless, nor blushing at your own avowed
Disgraceful idleness, that you have nought
To interest or amuse, when summer months
Forbid you through the forest or the field

To urge the devious chace, or weather foul
Prevents the intercourse of neighbours near.
Rouse from such mental torpor, & acquire, 310
In pity to your family & friends,
In pity to yourself, a better taste.
Let them not see you doze before the fire
In gloomy idleness, or pace the room
With restless irritation, & throw damp
On the domestic circle. – Do your part
To make home pleasant, & while fairer hands
Trace leaf & flower upon the muslin clear,
Break not the netting pin, nor seemly row
Derange, of bobbins pendant on the lace; 320
Scratch not the scissors on the table laid
Careless, & tempting to the idle hand,
And mar, by cutting into slips & shreds,
From mere vacuity of mind, & want
Of rational employment, female work;
But cheat their labours with the legend true
Of history, or Bard's fictitious tale.
  So let the evening pass, but for the day
More active occupation do you ask?
Some interesting object which may call 330
For a long morning's walk? Within your reach
Lies one, which duty claims; one, never yet
Pursued, without a blessing in its train.
"'Tis charity, my reader, charity."
Benevolent affections exercised
For all our fellow creatures. That alone
Can teach us to enjoy our happier lot.
Look from the gently rising knoll, where stands
Your mansion elegant, enriched with all
Those comforts truly English, which in vain 340
In other lands we look for, – Down the vale
Turn your attentive eye: how numerous rise
The cottages on either side the road!
Various in size & shape, but none secured
From the bleak winds, keen frosts, or driving hail,
Descending rapid from the wintry sky.
  Think, that in these abodes, no slender part
Of Britain's population must reside.
A hardy race, 'tis true, by habit long

Inured to bear the season's difference,   350
The "icy fang of winter", & the damps
Autumnal of the fast declining year,
With far less suffering than the nerves relaxed
By luxury & indolence; yet still
Remember they have feelings like your own;
And though in youth & health, they may not heed
Those numerous privations, which alas!
In every land on poverty attend;
Short is this season in the strongest frame,
Made shorter oft by labour premature,   360
Or late protracted; and th'alternate change
Sudden & frequent, from the burning blaze
Of harvest noons, to the night's chilling air.
Hence the rheumatic cramps, & aguish chill,
And fitful feverish heat – which call for food
More nourishing, for vestment warm, & all
Those little comforts, needed much
To solace sickness, but above the reach
Of daily labour's stipend to obtain.
On you, whose plenteous board their labours fill   370
With all its luxuries, they call for help;
Allow their claim, nor let them call in vain.
Leave not the sufferer to the pittance small,
Which all unwillingly the Vestry grant,
But from your ample store, impart whate'er
May comfort sickness – Nor your wealth
Alone bestow; it is small charity to part
With superfluity you cannot miss.
Give what may cost you something, time & thought.
'Tis not enough the pitcher's daily filled   380
With broth nutritious, or the skilful Leech
Sent from the neighbouring town, to prove what art
Medicinal, & potent drugs can do,
To renovate the exhausted frame. – Visit oft
Yourself, the poor man's cottage, nor disdain
To climb the narrow stair, which winding leads
Up to the chamber of the sick – there learn
Their real condition, & their numerous wants,
Which known & seen, you gladly would releive
But which unseen, would never strike the thought   390
Of those whom rank & affluence secure

From having felt themselves. – Your visit there
In person, & the interest it bespeaks,
In what concerns their welfare, will be felt
A greater kindness, than the best supply,
Which you can send by others for their wants.
Nor are such visits profitless to those
Who kindly make them; for true Charity
Like her twin sister Mercy, is *twice* bless'd:
She blesseth him that gives, & him that takes.　　　　　400
Hence is a lesson learn't, which more or less
All sometimes need. – A lesson of content
And thankfulness, for blessings manifold,
Which Providence with kind & liberal hand
Has given them to enjoy. Yet rarely known
Or valued as they ought, unless compared
With poverty's privations, wants & pains. –
Oft have I thought, (returning from the call
Which Duty bade me make) when I have marked
The hut, mud floored & damp, & thinly thatched;　　　410
The chamber without chimney, straw-stuffed bed
And curtainless – where lie the sick & old,
Though scant of comforts, uttering no complaint;
Yes, I have said, 'Oh! could the pampered sons
Of luxury & indulgence – thankless oft,
Nay worse than thankless – daring to complain
Of some imaginary good witheld,
Some self created want; scenes such as those
Once witness; – rising shame would do
Its proper office. – In their altered hearts　　　　　420
Excite a juster gratitude to Heaven.
Then selfishness, fallen nature's worst disgrace,
Would shrink abashed, & open leave the heart,
To kindliest feelings for another's pain.
　　　　One half the world, alas! but little know
The sufferings of the other. They who live
In cities least of all; for there the sight
Of poverty, & sickness & distress,
Intrudes not on the pleasures of the gay,
Or business of the busy. Alleys dark　　　　　　　　430
And garrets high, shut out their inmates poor
From public notice; & we walk the streets
Mids't glittering shops, & gay & well dres't crowds,

And equipages rich, till we forget
That sickness, pain & poverty exist
In this mix't world. And hence I deem it not
A small advantage in a country life
That from the daily labours & pursuits
Of either party, different as they are,
The poor are brought in contact with the rich.   440
If sickness keep the peasant from his work,
If from the barn, no falling flail is heard,
Nor sharper note of whetted scythe resounds
In field or garden; or the plough stands still;
His absence will be noticed. On his bed
He will not pine, unpitied or forgot,
But from his kind employer's willing hand
Will soon receive that help his need requires.

     But not to sickness be your care confined;   450
In health, promote the comforts of the poor,
Encourage as you can (& much you may)
The quiet & industrious. Praise bestow
Upon their cottage clean, & garden neat,
Their children orderly, & tightly clad.
To such, from the broad stripe of greensward waste
Which lines the road, a small allotment make,
Or in the fresh plantation's looser mould,
Or hedge row lately grubbed, allow them oft
To cultivate the farinaceous root
By Raleigh first imported; of more worth   460
Than all he sought for in Guyana's mines.
Find for the failing powers of tottering age
And tender hands of childhood, labours light,
Which call not for the vigor of life's prime.
The sand walk weeded, or the grassy swarth
Cut by the Gardener's scythe, from off the lawn
Swept clean; or Autumn's shower of withered leaves
Cleaned from the path, by brushwood overhung;
Or spray of elm removed, by rooks beat down
In airy fight contending for their nests;   470
Defacing else with litter, the green mead
And herbage springing fresh, will give an air
Of tidiness, to all your precincts round;
Will cost you little, yet do much for them:
Each slight increase of the week's earnings, adds

Some little comforts to their simple meal.

Yet let not honest but mistaken zeal
To lessen misery, degenerate
Into that easiness of temper weak,
Which gives to all that ask, however ill 480
They may deserve it. – Due distinction make,
Nor let the intemperate or dishonest, share
Your bounty; nor too credulous believe
Each piteous tale of whining discontent,
Or clamorous murmer, nor in haste releive
The wants brought on by thriftlessness or waste.
It may be well for them, & work perhaps
Some reformation, were they made to feel
The sufferings they have brought upon themselves.
This lesson taught, & symptoms once perceived 490
Of real penitence, encourage then –
But gradual, & with caution, the fair hope
They may regain your favour in due time;
And teach them, if they ever wish to win
Your kindness & support, they must deserve it.
Of such a system, steadily pursued,
The village quiet from disgraceful brawls,
And noisy shout of drunken revelry;
The ale house, reft of more than half its guests,
Would practically prove the benefit. 500
E'en the loose inmates of the hamlet small,
Whose straggling cottages the common edge,
Or forest devious boundary occupy,
The smugglers & the poacher's known abode,
Would humanise in time – be oft reclaimed
From their marauding lives, when taught to feel
What blessings wait on sober industry.

There want not many, well I know, who deem
Such efforts wholly useless; & contend
That gratitude is never to be found 510
In the unfeeling bosoms of the poor.
I would not think so, for ten thousand worlds,
Nor can I e'er beleive it – True it is
We sometimes meet with most unkind returns
For deeds of kindness to the poor performed;

111

And from their betters too: – In every rank
The selfish & the thankless will be found.
I know, (I am not blinded to their faults)
The pilfering hand will tear the shatter'd fence,
Will wrench the green limbs from the growing tree,   520
And in the garden depredation make,
Of him whose hand has fed them. Yet to tax
In one broad accusation, all the poor,
With general thanklessness, is most unfair,
Uncandid, & unjust. – Experience too,
Mine does at least, disproves the sweeping clause
Thus brought against nine tenths of all mankind.

    Long intercourse has led me to remark
In those who tread the humbler paths of life,
A difference of character as great   530
As marks the higher ranks. The rudest minds
Have sometimes softest feelings. I have known
Midst manners vulgar, & expressions coarse,
Awkwardly shown perchance, but yet sincere,
A pure & genuine thankfulness of heart.
One such I daily see; & though the mean
And vulgar annals of a peasant's life,
May draw on his Biographer a smile
Contemptuous from the critic, I will tell
The simple tale, & from oblivion save   540
The memory of an honest, grateful man.

    For many a year, upon our little farm
The plough he guided; & a master serv'd
Kind, liberal & good – he served my Father,
And served him with activity & zeal.
His master's interest was his own – his heart
Was ever in the field or in the Barn.
No other joy he wished for, than to see
His well conditioned team & thriving crops;
No other learning knew, than how to chalk   550
With figures no one but himself could read,
On his oak table, the last month's account;
Nor other dissipation knew, beyond
The yearly gala of a harvest home. –

Thus year succeeded year, & in due time
His temperate habits, & his frugal life,
Enabled him with provident forecast,
For helpless age, or children, to lay by
A sum, not trifling, for his modest wants.
But in a luckless hour he lent it all   560
To a fair spoken, speculative man,
Who broke, & fled his country; & a small
And paltry dividend was all he got.
What said he then? I do remember well –
He said, "I must forgive him," & he did.
I never heard him with intemperate rage
Abuse the wretch who wronged him. What he felt,
He felt in silence – lived as he was won't,
And patiently began a second hoard. –
Thus past some years succeeding – till at length   570
The farm was vacant, for my Father's age
Required rest, & so did honest John's.
To Bath removed my parent; ere he went
He for his faithful servant found a place
With a kind neighbour, who well knew his worth,
And placed him in a cottage tight & warm,
And gave him to direct & overlook
The labourers on a wide extended farm;
And to the weekly market, never failed
To send him with his sample – Office deemed   580
Of no small credit, dignity & trust.
And seemed it now, as if his future days
Would all pass quietly, without fresh change.
But human life, e'en in a peasant's cot
Exhibits many an unexpected turn.

One morn, (I shall not soon forget it) we were roused
By the loud cry of fire, & starting up
Beheld the cottage & adjacent barn
In one bright blaze. Already the thatch'd roof
Had disappeared – Along the rafters old,   590
Dry with the eastern breeze of windy March,
Quick ran the crackling flame. – Up rose the smoke,
In circling volumes – & a flashy shower
Of mingled sparks & ashes, far & wide
Dimm'd the dark sky, & fell o'er distant fields

Meanwhile the village crowd assembling round,
Had roused my good old neighbour from his bed
He, & his little family escaped
Unhurt, & there was time, & just enough
To have saved from the fast spreading flame,   600
His goods & chattels – But amongst this scene
Of wild confusion, he bethought him soon,
That in a shed contiguous to the barn,
Was lodg'd a fine & valuable colt,
A favourite of his Master's. – What to do
Was soon decided, & as soon performed.
He rush'd, with all th'activity of youth
Into the stall, & soon led out
The snorting, trembling animal – thus sav'd
His master's property, & left his own   610
To perish as it might; and so he lost,
His little all. For soon the smouldering cot,
And all within it, sank into a heap
Of burning ashes; and alone remained
An outside shell of black & dismal wall.
     'Tis somewhat late, at threescore years & ten,
To start afresh in life – to have a home
And house to look for; but he look'd not long:
For from that hour, (I claim no merit here,
What could I less?) I took him to my house,   620
And, like Orlando, nurtured the old age
Of this good Adam. – And now twelve years
Have almost slipp'd away, since he became
A thankful inmate of the Parsonage.
But ne'er shall I forget, when first I made
The welcome offer, what a grateful joy
His time worn features show'd. He started up,
And grasping my seized hand (I almost think
I feel the pressure, while I tell the tale)
"And will you, then God bless you Sir," he said.   630
Nor were these words the mere effusion quick
Of feeling. Rude & native eloquence
Here spoke the language of an honest heart;
And gave a pledge, which he has long redeem'd
By many a year's officious service done,
Such as a healthful & a green old age,
"Frosty, but kindly," can as yet perform.

An instance rare, I grant, my honest friend;
A character not easy to be match'd;
But one such proof of honest grateful zeal   640
To make requited, as his means afford,
For deeds of kindness, may excite a hope
That kind attentions are not always lost,
Whatever some suppose: nor let it here
Offend, if haply we should dare to hint
One error in the charity of those
Who really wish to be the poor man's friend,
But know not how; who with mistaken zeal
Releive the body, & neglect the mind.
If so, no marvel that their kindness fails   650
To meet a due return – In thankfulness,
Like other virtues, is the work of grace,
Not Nature – & he looks for it in vain,
Who thinks to find it in the heart of man,
Yet unenlightened by religious truth.
Oh! let us not forget the poor have souls
As well as bodies, nor suppose that vice
And ignorance are maladies, which call
Less loudly for relief, than pain or want.
Of small importance were it to secure,   660
E'en if we could secure (which cannot be,
For sin brings sufferings, which defy the power
Of charity to heal,) man's outward frame
From the destructive ravage of disease
Or poverty's privations, for some short
And quickly passing years; if careless still
Of his immortal spirit, we do nought
To save him from eternal misery. –
Oh! then, neglect not to disperse abroad
That sacred Volume, which alone contains   670
The Christian's charter'd rights to endless joys,
When this brief scene is over as it must,
Pass some few years, to all who tread life's stage.
Nor heedless to accompany the gift
With its legitimate companion; with its true
And genuine offspring. For derived from thence,
And breathing much its spirit, do I hold
The manual of our Church's holy rites.
The prayer book ever is the poor man's best

And safest comment on the Scripture text.   680
It is a quiet unobtrusive guide,
And by its temperate & yet fervent forms,
Its sound & scriptural doctrines, may preserve
From Calvinism's dark bewildering maze
And heart appalling views, the humble mind
Of the unletter'd Christian. – From the shelf
Which his small batter'd library contains,
Banish the fanatic, schismatic tract
Which monthly issues from th'all licensed press,
Stitched in blue paper; where in frontispiece   690
Stare the harsh features of some saintly man,
Some self appointed preacher of dissent,
Whose page too oft contains the poisonous creed
Of Antinomian error, or at best
Perverts the mind by the delusive hope
Of strong assurance inwards – & the tale,
The wondrous tale, of childhood's premature
Devout experience – tells the dying words
Of sucking confessors, & embryo saints.
Hence is the path way to the village fane   700
Untrodden – & the bells "have knolled to Church,"
Now all unheeded by the gifted swain.
Well meaning, but ill guided, off he goes
To the lone common's edge, where quaint & square
Stands the new Meeting house. There hears, half pleased,
And half appalled, & not half what he hears
Interpreting, the doctrines wild & strange
Of some itinerant pastor, who the fold
Has enter'd by the window, not the door:
Who makes the righteous sad by false alarms,   710
Or speaks of peace to hearts where peace is not;
And this he calls, "the *Gospel fully preach'd*."

13th. Psalm

Where Babel's stream its world of waters pours
O'er cultured plains, along its willowed shores
Mournful we sat; in fond remembrance dear
Our distant country caused the incessant tear;
While with loose cords neglected & unstrung
On every tree our silent harps were hung.
Our haughty conquerors called, but called in vain
For Judah's song, & Sion's holy strain.
Can exiles from their country far away,
Chaunt in a foreign soil their native lay?   10
Ah! no, Could I forget thy sacred towers,
Fair Salem, e'en in mirth's luxurious hours,
If I to them prefer a foreign land,
Mute be my tongue, & palsied be my hand.
     O'er you shall Heaven's remembered vengeance fall,
Children of Edom, deaf to friendship's call,
Who basely joined the fierce & pagan foe,
And urged them to Judea's overthrow.
Daughter of Babel, tremble at thy doom,
Soon shall thy day of retribution come.   20
The weeping Sires their murdered offspring see,
And injured Judah's wrongs be visited on thee.

Novr. 22^d. 1819

117

126th. Psalm

When Sion's tribes, at Heaven's command,
Who, exiled in a foreign land
Their long captivity had mourned,
To Judah's happy soil returned,
The scene scarce real could we deem,
But feared the whole some fond delusive dream.

2

What raptures then inspired each breast,
What grateful joy each voice expressed,
While thus we prayed with one accord;
"Turn our captivity Oh! Lord,   10
As southern torrents swollen with rain,
Flash o'er their beds, & drench the thirsty plain.

3

Repentant tears, like Spring showers cold,
Can fertilize the softened mould;
And he who now with tearful pain
Throws o'er the field prolific grain,
In time his labour's meed receives,
And comes not unadorned with Autumn's rustling sheaves.

Nov.r 22d. 1819

114th. Psalm

Saved from proud Egypt's plagues, & Egypt's toil,
When Jacob's house left Goshen's foreign soil,
Midst Judah's tribes Jehovah raised his throne,
And Israel's chosen people called his own.
The sea saw, that & fled, & now no more
Beats thy hoarse tide against the sounding shore,
And Jordan's river, with reverted force
Bade its swift waves run backwards to their source:
Surrounding mountains felt their bases rock,
And hillocks bounded, like the bounding flock.   10
What aileds't thee O! sea, that thus no more
Beats thy hoarse tide against the sounding shore?
And why does Jordan with reverted force,
Bid its swift waves run backward to their source?
Why from their base do airy mountains rock,
Why bound the hillocks like the bounding flock.
Yes, t'was well done. Let river, earth & sea
Conscious proclaim the present Deity.
Tremble all nature at that awful hour,
When great Jehovah manifests his power;   20
Who pours forth waters from the flinty hill,
And freshens arid plains with many a sparkling rill.

Œnigmas

A plain there is, by wood surrounded,
And little rising hillocks bounded,
Where Autumn's hues are never seen,
But one unfading tint of green
O'er all the level plain is spread,
And yet 'tis neither mown nor fed.
Of bird or beast, no cheerful sound
The silence breaks, that reigns around;
A scene for peaceful contemplation,
Did not, for idle recreation,   10
Or led by thirst of wealth or fame,
Man introduce war's desperate game.
Tis then a scene of loud alarm;
Uplifted then is many an arm,
And many a well directed blow,
The flying enemy lays low;
For great the hazards of the battle;
Quick fly the balls, the cannons rattle,
While standers by, to mark delight
The varying progress of the fight.   20
And hard it is in truth to say,
Which hath th'advantage of the day:
For though the victory one must yield,
Retires each party from the field;
And both, (whatever they pretend)
Are out of pocket at the end.

April 28^{th.}1819

2^{d.}

For honesty, to say the truth,
   I have but a bad name:
Yet my white hairs from giddy youth
   Respect might surely claim.

No seaman, (though I live on land)
    More often sets the sail,
Nor when he leaves his native strand
    More courts the rising gale.

That fortune is a changing jade
    Let others fear or feel;   10
I carry on a thriving trade,
    However turns the wheel.

The sexton's paid to toll the bell,
    By friends who still survive;
I for myself can toll full well,
    Or should not be alive.

3ʳᵈ.

In a tight little cottage, whose straw cover'd roof
Though humble & low, is at least weather proof,
I've resided for many long years with my wife,
And a pattern we sure are for conjugal life:
For between us, I venture to say was ne'er heard
A passionate quarrel, or single cross word.
Yet it is not because we're unknown or neglected,
For our motions have ever been closely inspected;
And our neighbours, in cases both doubtful & nice,
Would look in upon us, & ask our advice.   10
But fall'n is our credit, of late they apply
To another adviser, I cannot tell why:
'Tis perhaps love of change, or 'tis possibly pride,
For he certainly moves in a circle more wide;
And his mansion by far does out [sic] cottage surpass,
Adorned with mahogany, cut steel & glass:
But this is all show; I can make it appear
He has often deceived them this very last year:
And I think, if with treachery confidence ends,
They'll soon quit their new & consult their old friends.   20
But I must not add more, or too soon will be known
The name of our rival, at once & our own.

Singly, to possess my charms,
Soldiers fearless rush to arms,
Lawyers to their briefs apply,
Politicians scheme & lie,
Disregarding toil & scars,
And when they've gained me, bless their stars.
But when join'd with any other
Though it be my very Brother,
All my glory's banished quite,
We are then kept out of sight: 10
Modest ladies scarce will name us,
Though we made one lady famous;
Yet guess for once our names aright,
And, when you've got us, keep us tight.

5^(th).

Sure never was creature so grossly abused,
Of dullness more often or falsely accused:
For men of my service regardless, still dare
Each thick headed blockhead with me to compare;
Yet on many a trying & doubtful occasion
From me they are happy to gain information.
To my mind or my manners what can they object?
I ne'er domineer, though I love to direct.
On each race course I'm seen, but no mortal ere yet
Heard me take up the odds, or ere offer a bet.   10
Though my heart's tough as oak, yet my temper is quiet,
Yet I would not advise you unfairly to try it:
There is not much danger of my striking first,
But whoever attacks me will come off the worst.
Yet one fault I must own, of true cowards a mark,
I'm an enemy most to be fear'd in the dark –

6th.

If our company makes our true character known,
I scarcely know what I can say of my own;
For I'm often, my enemies truly alledge,
With gipsies so ragged found under a hedge;
Yet no party exists of the high & well dres't,
Who admittance refuse to so cheerful a guest;
But let me not boast, for my merits depend
After all, on the help of a snug little friend;
Indeed we are seldom apart, & no wonder,
For though cheerful apart, we are dull when asunder.   10
Though I live in a house that is close, dark & plain,
Yet a numerous circle I oft entertain;
I give them good fare, & produce butter'd pease
In all seasons, & roast beef whenever I please.
And my cellar you'll think must be well stocked & handy,
For when called for, I always bring out drops of brandy.

7th.

Of strange & compound form am I;
Part once in Palestine wav'd high,
    As sacred writers tell;
And part in England's north had birth,
A tourist writes, who knew my worth,
    And always used me well.

Though sceptic Whigs pronounced it trick,
With royal touch Anne cured the sick,
    And cleared their scurvy faces:
My touch far more effective proves,   10
Pimples & spots at once removes,
    And gives unfading graces.

To hundreds I give fame & bread,
But ill my services are paid,
    I speak it to my sorrow;
For why, I cannot understand,
To-day who take me by the hand,
    Will cut me on the morrow –

8th.

Peg Nicholsons & Sheriff Knights stand by;
A Knight of more antiquity am I.
My weight & worth through England is confest
And I am well, though always plainly drest.
Loved by the Mob – I yet make no confusion
But well support the British Constitution.
Such are my merits – let my faults be known
With Sermons I am easily o'erdone
And when long winded Preachers show no quarter
I make some other people wish them shorter   10
Another failing my best friends discern
When once set on, I'm rather hard to turn
Take one hint more & all my faults are told
Who love me best, will often find me cold

9th.

Divided, of an ancient house am I,
A long, & dark, & sometimes useless story:
United, I declare the station high,
Of those who best support old England's glory.

Charades

1st.

By all prudent folks, he a rash man is reckoned,
Who before he has gotten my first, takes my second:
Yet my first will afford him but little delight,
To the name of my whole, if my second's in sight.

2nd.

In my first, that he may not be tardy or late
My second to do, & make nobody wait,
      A Curate oft crosses the plain:
But if to my whole, he should ever advance,
To me it appears an improbable chance
      He should ever do either again.

3rd.

If there be truth in proverbs old, my first
Is best of servants, but of masters worst.
Ruin unlimited my second brings,
Thus flushed with triumph, knaves exult o'er kings.,
My whole a different sight more grateful gave;
Saw kings victorious, & a conquer'd knave.

My First a Horseman's dire disgrace would tell
If it were only longer by an *L*. –
My next, if strong enough, and not too short
Will always prove old age's best support;
But much I doubt if any living Wight
Can well support my whole for one short night.

My first can well finish a bottle of Wine
    But will never another begin
My second's large belly, if right I opine
    Can a much larger portion take in,

They who live at my whole, though sent there to drink nought
    But large draughts from Castalia's rill;
Are suspected to swallow more wine than they ought
    As their parents find out by their bill

J.A.

My 2^{d} may in youth be very charming
But in old age is horribly alarming;
And therefore, (if to speak the truth I durst)
My 2^{d} oft resolves to be my First;
Nay, loves to be my whole; for that they say,
Leads to my first, & at no distant day –

BIBLIOGRAPHY

Unpublished

Chawton   4to volume. watermarks 1834 and 1835, in hand of Anna Lefroy, containing poetry by James Austen, as well as drawings (by Anna), answers to the enigmas, James's speech to the Basingstoke Branch of the SPCK and, appended at the back, a few other items not in her hand. Jane Austen Memorial Trust. Chawton.

Chute   Album of word-games in hand of Elizabeth Chute. Hampshire Record Office, Austen-Leigh archive 23M93/70/4.

Gilson   Small album in unidentified hand, c.1830, containing 44 riddles and charades by members of the Austen family. Also other MSS. David Gilson Esq.

HRO   4to volume, watermark 1834, in hand of Caroline Mary Craven Austen [?], containing poetry by James Austen. Hampshire Record Office, Austen-Leigh archive 23M93/60/3/2. Other MSS and microfiches in same archive.

HRO MS   4to sheets containing copies of poetry by James Austen (some incomplete) in unknown hand; watermarks 1802 and 1813. Hampshire Record Office, Austen-Leigh archive 23M93/60/3/1.

Isel   4to volume, watermark 1827, possibly in hand of James Edward Austen-Leigh. The first 16 poems are in a large, ornate hand with elaborate titles. Some texts have lines numbered (in 10s). There is an Index at the front. Isel Hall, Cumbria.

Published

All references to the novels of Jane Austen are to the Oxford Illustrated Jane Austen, ed. R.W. Chapman, Oxford, 1923. The Juvenilia and other minor works were first collected in vol.VI of the Oxford edition as *Minor Works*, ed. Chapman, 1954, rev. B.C. Southam, 1969.

References to *Jane Austen's Letters* are to the 3rd edition, ed. Deirdre Le Faye, Oxford, 1995.

Austen, Caroline Mary Craven, *My Aunt Jane Austen,* Jane Austen Society, 1952.

—, *Reminiscences of Caroline Austen,* ed. Deirdre Le Faye, Jane Austen Society, 1986.

Austen-Leigh, J.E, *A Memoir of Jane Austen*, London, 1870.

— *Recollections of the Early Days of the Vine Hunt*, London, 1865.

Austen Leigh, Mary Augusta, *James Edward Austen Leigh: A Memoir*, privately printed, 1911.

Austen-Leigh, R.A., *Austen Papers*, London, 1942.

Austen-Leigh, W., Austen-Leigh, R.A., and Le Faye, Deirdre, *Jane Austen: A Family Record*, London, 1989.

Honan, Park, *Jane Austen: Her Life*, London, New York, 1987

Jane Austen Society, *Collected Reports*, 4 vols, 1949-95; continuing.

Lane, Maggie, *Jane Austen's Family: Through Five Generations*, London, 1984.

Le Faye, Deirdre, *Jane Austen's 'Outlandish Cousin': The Life and Letters of Eliza de Feuillide*, London, 2002.

Selwyn, David, ed., *Jane Austen: Collected Poems and verse of the Austen family*, Manchester, 1996.

Tucker, George Holbert, *A Goodly Heritage: A History of Jane Austen's Family*, Manchester, 1983.

TEXTUAL NOTES

1   AN EPISTLE TO FULWAR CRAVEN FOWLE ESQ^R. 1780.
Source: Chawton
Variants in Isel:
No stanza divisions
Title *Curate* Clergyman
21   *vales* Vale
25   *tired* fired
29   *worn* worse
30   *Naïds* Naiads
51   *Forbade* Forbad

3   AN ELEGY WRITTEN AT KINTBURY BERKS 1781. Source: Chawton

5   THE HERMIT 1781. Source: Chawton
Variants in Isel:
28   *beechen* beachen
30   *fulfill* fulfil
35   *shrubby* shrubly
38   *round* around
49   *noon tide* midday
59   *o'erhang* o'ercharge
61   *chearful* cheerful
65   *Re echo* Re-echoes
90   *still pours an artless note* still pours in artless note
96   *crowd* croud

8   PROLOGUE TO THE TRAGEDY OF MATILDA 1782. Source: HRO
Variants in Chawton and Isel:
Title *acted at Steventon Hants* acted at Steventon 1782 (Ch)
    Edward Austen Edwd. Austen [in pencil: afterwards Knight] (Ch)
6   *lightening* Lightning (I)
8   *pease* Rase [i.e. 'scratch'; but presumably a miscopying of 'Pease'] (I)
9   *Hero's* Heroe's (I)
12   *crowd* croud (I)
28   *galleries* Gallery (Ch, I)
Below: Æta 17 (Ch); Æt 17 (I)

9   EPILOGUE TO THE TRAGEDY OF MATILDA 1782. Source: Chawton
Variants in Isel:
5   *what* when
8   *or* of

10   PROLOGUE TO THE RIVALS 1784. Source: HRO
Variants in Chawton and Isel:
Title *Prologue to The Rivals* Prologue to the Rivals Comedy By Sheridan (I)
Acted by some young Ladies and Gentlemen at Steventon acted at Steventon
1784 (Ch)
H. Austen Henry Thos. Austen (Ch)
14   *shaft* shafts (Ch)
15   *show* shew (Ch) *dres't* dressed (Ch)
22   *wait* court (Ch)
23   *in* when (Ch)

11   EPILOGUE TO THE RIVALS 1784. Source: Chawton
Variants in Isel:
8   *when* where
16   *Counsels!* Council!

11   THE RASH RESOLUTION 1784. Source: Gilson

14   SONNET TO LADY CATHERINE POWLET 1785. Source: Chawton

14   SONNET TO WINTER 1785. Source: Chawton
Variants in Isel:
Lines 2 3 6 7 10 11 13 indented

15   SONNET TO SPRING 1785. Source: Chawton
Variants in Isel:
Lines 2 3 6 7 10 12 14 indented

15   SONNET TO AUTUMN 1785. Source: Chawton
Variants in Isel:
Lines 2 3 6 7 10 12 14 indented
10   *nor* or

16   SONNET TO SUMMER 1785. Source: Chawion
Variants in Isel:
Lines indented alternately

16   SONNET ON LEAVING OXFORD 1785. Source: Chawton

17   LINES ADDRESSED TO MISS CHARLOTTE BRYDGES 1786.
Source: Chawton
Variants in Isel: Seven four-line stanzas, numbered
Title *Lines Addressed to* Lines To
6   *Must – power* Must -'s Power
10   *least* lest

17 SONNET TO THE SAME 1786. Source: Chawton

18 PROLOGUE TO THE WONDER 1787. Source: HRO
Variants in Chawton and Isel:
Title *Decr: 28th: & 29th:* the 26th. & 28th. of December (Ch)
2   *her* the (Ch)
18 *time* hours (Ch, I)
24 *Pageants* pageant (Ch)
26 *policy* politics (Ch, I)
42 *smile* Face (I)
Below: J Austen (I)

20 EPILOGUE TO THE COMEDY OF TIIE WONDER 1787. Source: HRO
Variants in Chawton and Isel:
Title HRO has, erroneously, Tragedy. Place and dates of acting omitted in Ch.
2   *Rose ...night* "Rose ... Night" (I)
3   *bade* bad (1)
10 *Losing* Loving (Ch, I)
15 *whilst* While (Ch)
17 *with ... pride* (With ... Pride) (I)
20 *That called* And styled (Ch, I)
29 *its* their (Ch, I)
37 *jealousy* Jeaulously [sic] (I)
41 *bands* bonds (Ch, I)

21 PROLOGUE TO THE CHANCES 1788. Source: HRO
Variants in Chawton and Isel:
5   *dres't* dressed (I)
8   *the minds of tender youth* the mind of tender youth (I) the early mind of youth (Ch)
32 *bowers* hours (Ch, I)
44 *shal't* shall (I)
45 *For* Too (I) *near* ne'er (Ch, I)
46 *or* & (Ch, I)
51 *thine* thy (Ch)
53 *where* when (Ch) *wher'ere* when'ere (Ch) whene'er (I)
57 *Paine* Payne (Ch) *pours* pores (Ch, I)
64 *For we alas! ourselves* For we ourselves Alas! (Ch, I)

23 PROLOGUE TO THE TRAGEDY OF TOM THUMB 1788. Source: HRO
Variants in Chawton and Isel:
3   *Britains* Britons (Ch, 1)
6   *do but* do not (Ch)
12 *favourite* favorite (1)

14 *intent* effects (I)
23 *time* hours (Ch, I)
24 *practise* practice (Ch) *haloo* hallow (I)
32 *fall'n* fallen (Ch, I)
36 *crowd* croud (I)
49 *supplies* [altered in HRO from supplys]
50 *December's* December (Ch, I)
51 *on kimbo* or kembow (I)
54 *soothe* sooth (Ch, I)
56 *wealth & liberty* Liberty & Wealth (Ch, I)
59 *us* as [sic] (I)
66 *downs* down (Ch, I)
69 *joys* joy (Ch, I) ·
77 *Cheered* Cheared (Ch)
78 *&* or (Ch, I)
85 *sit* set (I)
100 *resistless power may boast* a power resistless boast (Ch, I)
103 *the unfinished work* th'unfinished work (Ch, I)
117 *pourtrayed [displayed* cancelled] portrayed (Ch, I)
121 *crowd* croud (I)
123 *favourite* favorite (I)
124 *approving* applauding (I)

26 PROLOGUE TO A PRIVATE THEATRICAL EXHIBITION 1788
Source: HRO
Variants in Chawton and Isel:
7 *their* the (Ch)
18 *cornucopiae* Cornucopias (Ch)
19 *power* hand (Ch, I)
26 *Bess's* Besse's (I)
32 *did* does (Ch, I)
34 *clue* clew (Ch, I)
42 *parts* part (Ch, I) *care* ease (Ch)
47 *has* he's (Ch)
51 *scene* stage (Ch, I)
54 *wives* [omitted in I]
58 *Actors* acting (Ch)

27 EPILOGUE TO THE SULTAN 1790. Source: HRO
Variants in Chawton and Isel:
Title [MS has Miss C–] *in the character of Roxalana* as Roxalana (Ch)
5 *the best of all rules* that best of all rules (Ch, I)
13 *tied* tried (Ch, I)
24 *I'm* I am (I)

26   *I did* did 1 (Ch,I)
34   *as* what (I)
35   *beleive* believe (Ch, I)
41   *tried* tryed (I)
48   *Viziers* Vizier (Ch, I)
53   *honour* honor (Ch, I)
Below: I(I)

29   THE MAID OF THE MOOR 1802[?]. Source: HRO MS

33   APRIL 1805 TO MARY   1805. Source: HRO
Variants in Chawton and Isel:
Lines 2 3 6 8 of each stanza indented (I)
Title April (Ch) April to Mary (I)
9   *landscape* landskip (I)
10   *rattling sleet & hail* sleet & rattling hail (Ch)
14   *that* which (Ch)
16   *vernal* early (Ch)
24   *delight* rejoice (Ch, I)
26   *nor* or (Ch)
28   *the horizon's* th'horizon's (Ch)
47   *Within man's breast alternate reign* Within Man's heart altogether reign (Ch)
Below: April 29 1805 (Ch) April 29th 1805 (I)

35   TO EDWARD ON THE DEATH OF HIS FIRST PONY 1811. Source: HRO
Variants in Chawton and Isel:
Title No date (Ch, I)
3-33 Speech marks at the beginning of lines (Ch)
8-9   Lines reversed (Ch)
12   *saintefoin* sainfoin (Ch, I)
17   *shun* shewn (Ch)
18   *But* Yet (Ch, I)
40   *son* boy (Ch, I)
42   Speech marks at the beginning of lines
50   *lively* kindly (Ch)
51   *awhile* a while (I)
54   *on* in (Ch)
60   *wearied* tried (Ch) tired (I)
63   *&* or (Ch, I)
64   *would* could (I)
67   Bracket not in Ch or I and obviously a mistake
70   *quadraped* Quadrupede (Ch) Quadruped (I)
84   *sure* soon (Ch)

94   *held* hold (Ch)
106   *each* such (Ch)
Below: Jany 1811 (Ch)

37   TO CAROLINA – ON HER BIRTHDAY 1811. Source: HRO
Variants in Chawton and Isel:
Title No date (Ch, I)
4   *existence* existance (I)
11   *smoothe* smooth (Ch, I)
12   *favourite's* favorite's (I)
19   He *may grant* As He may grant (Ch, I [cancelled in HR])
21   *lapsed* passed (Ch)
40   *Fear* Fears (Ch, 1)
46   *misled* undone (Ch, I)
66   *infant* early (I)
Below: June 18 1811 (Ch) June 18th. 1811(I)

39   TO MISS JANE AUSTEN THE REPUTED AUTHOR OF SENSE AND
   SENSIBILITY 1811 [?]
Source: Gilson MS
This verse, in a disguised hand, is attributed to James Austen by Deirdre Le
Faye (see *Jane Austen: A Family Record* (London, 1989), p.168. The date is
conjectural from the first publication of *S&S*.

39   TO MARY, ON HER WEDDING DAY 1812. Source: HRO
Variants in Chawton and Isel:
Title No date (Ch, I)
2   *passed* slipped (Ch, I)
6   *fallen* fall'n (Ch, I)
7   *cheering* chearing (I)
21   *rain* hail (Ch, I)
32   *oppres't* oppressed (Ch)
40   *landscape* landskip (I)
41   *expres't* expressed (Ch)
53   *cheerful* chearful (Ch, I)
Below: January 17th (Ch, I)

41   LINES WRITTEN AT KINTBURY 1812. Source: HRO MS
Copy in Chawton ends at 1.98.
Variants in HRO (album), Chawton and Isel:
Title Written at Kintbury (Ch)
3   *brighter* lighter (HRO, I)
5   *'Midst scenes, whose varied landscape* In that fair spot, whose landscape
   (HRO)

6   *th'unsated* the unsated (HRO, I)
9   *tint* tints (HRO)
10   *grey* gray (Ch)
19   *Village* distant (HRO)
42   *sober'r* sober (HRO, I) soberer (Ch)
43   *live* lives (HRO, I)
44   *chuse* choose (HRO)
47   *mixed* mix't (HRO) mixt (Ch, I) *sensation* sensations (HRO, I)
50   *other* former (HRO)
58   *chearful* cheerful (I)
66   *savoury* sav'ry (HRO)
68   *Heightened* Heighten (HRO)
85   *plan'd* plann'd (HRO) planned (Ch)
87   *past* passed (Ch)
102 *Poet's* [omitted in I]
107 *remembrance* rememberance (HRO, I) *retrace* trace (HRO)
114 *and not know half* yet not know all (HRO)

44   HOME 1812. Source: HRO
Variants in Chawton and Isel:
2   *When* Where (Ch)
10   *Or* And (Ch, I)
35   *height* heigth (Ch)
41   *clothes* cloathes (I)
43   *verdant* oderous (Ch) odorous (I)
61   *height* heigth (Ch)
73   *eyes* eye (I)
Below: Septr. 1812 (Ch) September 1812 (I)

46   SELBOURNE HANGER 1812. Source: HRO MS
Variants in HRO (album), Chawton and Isel:
Title Selborne Hanger Nov^r: 18th. 1812 (HRO) Selbourn Hanger (Ch, I)
1   [*view* MS actually has *visit* but HRO, Ch and I all have view and it is so
    obviously copied in error that I have amended it.]
    Selbourne Selborne (HRO) Selbourn (Ch, I)
11   *It's* The (HRO, Ch, I)
31   *speck* spot (HRO,Ch, I)
32   *Wolmer* Wolmar (HRO)
33   *days* years (HRO, Ch, I)
38   *Headly's* Headleys's (HRO, I)
40   *the Horizons* th'horizon's (HRO, Ch, I)
45   *chearful* cheerful (HRO, I)
54   *Brings* Bring (Ch, I)
61   *Chaunted* Chanted (HRO)

65 *cloister's* cloistered (HRO)
69 *hour* hours (Ch)
73 *on* in (HRO, I)
77 *found* sought (HRO, Ch, I)
96 *awful* aweful (Ch, I)
97 *the* The (HRO, Ch,I)
104 *croud* crowd (Ch)
108 *secrecy* scenery (HRO, Ch, I)
109 *cloister'd* cloistered (HRO, Ch, I)
111 *vallies* valleys (HRO, Ch, I)
124 *reflection's* reflexion's (HRO)
126 *which* that (HRO, Ch, I)
140 *tastes* taste (HRO, Ch, I)
146 *Lordly* wealthy(HRO, Ch, I)
153 *Selbourne's* Selborne's (HRO)
155 *he was* was he (HRO, Ch, I)
156 *gift* gift[s?] (Ch)
159 *the enquiring* th'enquiring (HRO, Ch, I)
160 *and find* and ever find [ever added superscript] (Ch)
177 *charms* charm (Ch)
187 *Selbourne* Selborne (HRO)
Below: Initials and date not in HRO; date only in Ch and I.

51 TYGER'S LETTER TO CAROLINE 1812. Source: Chawton
Variants in HRO and Isel:
Tiger for *Tyger* throughout in HRO
7 *Believe* Beleive (HRO, I)
8 *spoilt* spoiled (HRO)
12 *Betsey* Betsy (HRO)
17 *her* the (HRO, I)

52 ADDRESS TO TYGER 1812. Source: Chawton
Variants in HRO and Isel:
Tiger for *Tyger* throughout in HRO
Title *the author's luncheon* my luncheon (HRO, I) no date in HRO and I
10 *Micænas* Micenas (HRO) Mecænas (I)
18 *Since* If (HRO)
24 *favorite* favourite (HRO)
25 *mere* meer (I)
35 *pur* purr (HRO)
43 Corbet's Corbet (HRO, I)
49 *Midst* 'Mongst (HRO, I) *weazels* weasels (HRO)
50 *lesson* terror (HRO, I)
Below: No date in HRO

53 TO EDWARD ON PLANTING A LIME TREE 1813. Source: HRO
Variants in Chawton and Isel:
Title *January 1813* Jany 1813 (Chawton)
10 *farewell* farewel (Ch, I)
27 *cheerful* chearful (Ch, I)
30 *each* the (Ch)
44 *health's* health (I)
65 *calm & pure* pure & calm (Ch, I)
76 *visit* visits (Ch)
82 *you* you've (Ch)
85 *cheerful* chearful (Ch, I)
87 *favourite* favorite (Ch, I)
88 *marked* mark'd (Ch)
95 *eyes* eye (Ch, I)
99 *found* known [clearly a miscopying] (Ch)
104 *the* this (Ch)
110 *On* Of (Ch, I)
112 *might* may (I)
Below: Jan^Y 1813 (Ch) January 1813 (I)

56 ULYSSES ANNOUNCES TO HECUBA THAT THE MANES OF
ACHILLES DEMAND THE SACRIFICE OF POLYXENA 1813[?].
Source: HRO MS
There is no evidence that James Austen is the author of this poem except for
its inclusion in the HRO MS. (For James Edward Austen-Leigh's poem on the
same theme, see Explanatory Notes.)

60 MORNING – TO EDWARD 1814 Source: HRO MS incomplete; HRO
(album) from l.123
Variants in HRO (album), Chawton and Isel:
Title April 11th. 1814 (HRO)
2 *daily* dayly (I)
10 *yeild* yield (HRO)
12 *chearful* cheerful (HRO)
21 *labour* labour[s?] (HRO)
24 *sleep* sloth (HRO)
26 *receive* receives (HRO, Ch, I)
28 *chearfully* cheerfully (HRO)
32 *Tenth* rest (HRO)
50 *or* & (HRO, Ch, I)
53 *cloath'd* clothed (HRO, Ch)
55 *chearless* cheerless (HRO, Ch)
58 *stopped* stuffed (HRO)

60   *and want, and age* & wants of age (HRO)
61   *They feel and own* They freely own (HRO, Ch, I)
63   *time* youth (HRO, Ch, I)
66   *Whose duty called for* Whose place demanded (HRO)
70   *time* place (Ch, I)
77   *chear* cheer (HRO, Ch, I)
82   *diversion* exertion (HRO) divertion (I)
83   *or* & (HRO, Ch, I)
87   *in truth* indeed (HRO)
88   *where* when (HRO, Ch, 1)
90   *where* when (HRO, Ch, I)
93-4 [omitted in HRO MS – on page turn]
99   *Grecians* Græcians (I)
100 *or* & (HRO, Ch)
105 *tost* tossed (HRO)
110 *labour* labours (HRO, Ch, I)
115 *satire* satyre (HRO, Ch, I)
121 *are* were (HRO, Ch, I)
131 *Defends* Maintains (Ch, I)
136-7 [omitted in HRO MS, HRO and I]
150 *symptoms* sympthoms (Ch) *foretel* foretell (Ch, I)
152 *fowls* Fowle's (I)
154 [Inserted at this point in Ch on a scrap of paper:
        In Pope's satyric verse is seen
        Horace – but Horace in the spleen;
        More pleasingly we trace him still
        In Cowper's lines to Joseph Hill.
        It's charm too, modern conversation]
183 *chief* sole (I)
185 *November's* December's (Ch, I)
186 *hills* fields (Ch, I)
198 *have* are (Ch, I)
199 *strength* youth (Ch, I)
203 *tremble* temble [sic] (I)
207 *passed* past (Ch, I)
212 *show* speak (Ch, I)
Below: April 11th. 1814 (Ch, I)

65   EVENING – TO EDWARD 1814. Source: Chawton
Variants in Isel:
Lines 2 and 5 indented in each stanza
14   *pudding or cabbage* cabbage or pudding
40   *chilly* chearless
46   *slipped* slips [slipped cancelled]

48   *gray* grey
55   *thankfully* chearfully

67   ON REFUSING A SPECIAL INVITATION 1814. Source: HRO
Variants in Chawton and Isel:
Lines 3 and 6 indented in each stanza (Ch, I)
Title *hounds at Mr Villebois Cover* hounds, which were to meet at Mr. Villebois's
    cover (Ch) hounds, which were to meet at Mr. Villeboy's cover (I)
    [Inserted in Ch on a scrap of paper: The writer, though in early youth a
    bold rider & addicted to Fox hunting had for many years given up the
    amusement; yet, when his son was old enough to mount a pony & follow
    the Hounds, he, for one or two seasons thought proper to accompany
    him –]
1   *morn* day (I)
5   *completely* compleatly (I)
17   *head* lead (Ch, I)
29   *sainfoin* saintfoin (Ch)
48   *halloo* holloo (I)
49   *meantime* meanwhile (Ch, I)
54   *Doctor* D^r. (Ch, I)
56   *Horner* Homer (I) [unclear in Ch]
71   *past* passed (I)
72   *never more* ne'er again (Ch, I)
Below: May 18th. 1814 (Ch, I)

70   LINES WRITTEN AT STEVENTON 1814. Source: HRO MS incomplete;
    HRO (album) to 1.130
Variants in HRO, Chawton and Isel:
4   *once* late (Ch, I)
17   *views* view (Ch, I)
20   *should I have* I should have (Ch, I)
34   *Receding* Receeding (Ch, I)
38   *felt* fell (Ch)
48   *nor* or (Ch, I)
55   *able* equal (Ch, I)
59   *daily* dayly (I)
65   *Thus sure would say* This sure w^d. say (Ch)
70   *to* with (Ch, I)
75   *neighbours* neighbour (Ch, I)
78   *borne* born (I)
86   *complete* compleat (Ch)
113   *stand* place (Ch, I)
125   *satire* satyre (Ch, I)
160   *or* and (HRO)

162 *boggy lane and miry field* miry field, & boggy lane (HRO)
163 *chearing* cheering (HRO)
176 *downwards* downward (HRO, I) *sprang* sprung (HRO)
188 *bank* banks (HRO, I)
189 *And shades* Shading (HRO)
192 *ozier* osier (HRO, Ch, I)
194 *Staind* Stained (HRO, Ch, I) *loomy* loamy (HRO, Ch, I)
195 *Charwell* Cherwell (HRO, Ch, I))
200 *transplanted* transported (HRO, Ch)
204-5 [omitted in Ch]
204 *chearful* cheerful (HRO)
205 *noontide* noontide's (HRO)
209 *chearful* cheerful (HRO, Ch)
211 *humbler style* humble stile (HRO, Ch, I)
227 *blasts* blast (HRO, I)
234 *terrass* terrace (HRO, Ch)
237 *ascend* [-ing cancelled in Ch]
240 *gabel* gable (HRO, Ch, I)
241 *above* amid (HRO)
243 *Is seen* I see (HRO, Ch, I)
245 *and* or (HRO, Ch, I)
252 *wall* walls (HRO)
253 *parasytic* [y cancelled, i substituted in I]
269 [omitted in HRO]
272 *heights* hills (HRO, Ch, I)
273 *vallies* valleys (HRO, Ch, I)
279 *the* this (HRO, Ch, I)
Below: July 1814 (I) [The date contradicts the title; it is likely that the offer of
the living was made in July and the poem written some months later, as is
suggested by the phrase 'as once I feared' in 1.4.]

77 AUTUMN 1815. Source: HRO MS incomplete; HRO (album) from 1.128
Variants in HRO (album), Chawton and Isel:
Title Autumn 1815 (HRO)
11 *brimstone* brimstone's (HRO)
14 *of* in (HRO, Ch, I)
15 *Britain's* British (HRO, Ch, I)
17 *chearful* cheerful (HRO)
26 *brought* taught (HRO, Ch, I)
27 *mixt* mixed (HRO, Ch, I)
30 *Æther* ether (HRO)
32 *mixt* mixed (HRO, Ch, I)
37 *croud* crowd (HRO, Ch, I)
44 *the* their (HRO, Ch, I)

45   *of* in [of erased] (HRO)
50   *ruddier* ruddy (HRO, Ch, I) *leaf* leafe (I)
83-6 [omitted in HRO MS; inserted in margin in HRO (album)]
83   *month* [omitted in HRO]
95   *weeder* weeders (HRO, Ch, I)
99   *gleam's* gloom (HRO, Ch, I)
101 *full* [erased in HRO]
102 *That croud* crowding (HRO) crowd (Ch)
133 *th'instructive* the instructive (Ch)
138 *daily* dayly (I)
170 *region* regions (Ch)
193-200 [Pencil addition in margin of Ch: Borrowed for Spring-tide]
196 *form* plant (Ch, I)
201 *hazles* hazels (Ch, I)
Below: January 24 - 1815 (I) [date cut off at foot of page in Ch]

83   THE AUTUMN WALK – TO MARY 1816. Source: Chawton
Variants in Isel:
10   *vapoury* vapory
12   *foss* fosse
15   *cheerless* chearless
26   *Gypsy's* Gypsie's
47   *tawny* tawney
52   *homeward* homewards
89   *Britania's* Britannia's
114 *interrupt* interupt
127 *cheerful* chearful
[Below in Ch: In order of time these lines should have been inserted before the last –]

86   'VENTA! WITHIN THY SACRED FANE' 1817. Source: autograph MS in the possession of the Warden and Fellows' Library, Winchester College, where there is a second copy, possibly in the hand of Henry Thomas Austen. There are also copies, with variants, in HRO and Isel. This is the only poem known to exist in James Austen's hand.
Significant variants:
Title *Lines* To the memory of his sister, Jane Austen, who died at Winchester, July 18th. 1817, & was buried in that Cathedral (HRO)
72   *Angles* [sic; corrected in copies]
74   *attendant* [possibly a mistake deriving from 1.68; copies substitute eternal]

88   LINES WRITTEN IN THE AUTUMN OF 1817 AFTER A RECOVERY FROM SICKNESS 1817. Source: HRO
Variants in Chawton and Isel:

7   *rustling* russling (I)
28   *cheerful* chearful (Ch, I)
33   *swell* swells (1)
41   *releives* relieves (Ch, I)
43   *clothes* clothe (Ch) cloath (I)
48   *overhanging* o'erhanging (Ch, I)
52   *cheers* chears (I)
77   *irresistible* irresistable (Ch) irrisistable (I)
83   *separate* seperate (I)
87   *sculls* skulls (Ch, I)
100 *interruption* interuption (I)
102 *Heav'n* Heaven (I)
104 *manifold* manyfold (Ch, I)
111 *garments* garment (Ch, I)
116 *How* For (Ch)
122 *buoyant* boyant (I)
123 *thoughtlessness* thoughtlesness (I)
124 *Uninterrupted* Uninterupted (I)
132 *Oh!* Ah! (I)
142 *Cleansed* Cleared (Ch, I)
154 *incompatible* incompatable (I)
178 *blinding* [overwritten] blinded (Ch, I)
183 *force* powers (Ch, I)
189 *thought* care (Ch, I)
190 *care* thought (Ch, I)
191 *hopes* hope (Ch, I)
195 *pertinaciously* pertinaceously (Ch)
203 *cheerful* chearful (Ch, I)
221 *faltering* faultering (Ch, I)
238 *occupation* occupations (Ch)
243 *characters* Character (I)
247 *unblameable* unblamable (I)
261 *Linnean* Linnæan (Ch, I)
268 *choose* chuse (Ch, I)
271 *boasts* boast (Ch)
274 *crowd* croud (I)
276 *hues* scenes (Ch)
286 *charms* charm (Ch, I)
291 *hazle* hazel (Ch, I)
300 *Lord of all I see around* Lord of almost all I see (Ch, I)
308 *foliage* herbage (Ch, I)
323 *where* when (Ch)
332 *side* hand (Ch, I)
336 *Britannia's* Britania's (Ch)

341 *pause* muse (Ch, I)
343 [*often* omitted in Ch]
348 *crop* graze (I)
352 *num'rous* numerous (Ch, I)
355 *whatsoever* whatever (Ch) *deem* [dream?] (I)
359 *encrease* increase (Ch, I)
374 *mere* meer (Ch, I)
386 *surprised* surprized (Ch, I)
391 *how* Now (Ch)
394 *hues* hue (Ch, I)
415 *Showed* Shewed (Ch, I)
431 *cheerless* chearless (I)
434 *cheerful* chearful (Ch, I)

99   THE ŒCONOMY OF RURAL LIFE 1819. Source: HRO
The last line is erroneously numbered 849; in fact it is 1.712.
9   [din was anticipated in error and later erased: the correct noun was not
     however inserted.]

117   137ᵀᴴ. PSALM 1819. Source:HRO
Variants in Chawton and Isel:
2   [*along* cancelled in Ch; cancelled and rewritten in I]
13   *them* thee (Ch)
18   *Judea's* Judæa's (I)
Date: Sunday Novʳ. 21ˢᵗ· 1819 (Ch, I)

118   126ᵀᴴ. PSALM 1819. Source: HRO
Variants in Chawton and Isel:
No verse nos. in Chawton
Title Psalm 126 (Ch)
12   *Flash* Rush (Ch)

119   114ᵗʰ. PSALM 1819. Source: HRO
Variants in Chawton and Isel:
Title Psalm 114 (Ch)
8   *backwards* backward (Ch)
11   *aileds't* ailest (Ch).

120   'A PLAIN THERE IS' 1819. Source: HRO
Variants in Chawton and Isel:
5   *plain* vale (I)
8   *that* which (Ch, I)
21   *And hard it is in truth to say* And hard in truth it is to say (Ch, I)
Date: April 28 1819 (I)

120 'FOR HONESTY, TO SAY THE TRUTH' Source: HRO
Variants in Chawton, Isel and Gilson:
12 *However* Whoever (G)
14 *still* yet (I, G)

121 'IN A TIGHT LITTLE COTTAGE' Source: HRO
Variants in Chawton, Isel and Gilson:
1 *cover'd* covered (Ch, I, G)
6 *quarrel* squabble (Ch, G) *or* a (G)
8 [*been* repeated in G] *closely* duly (Ch, G)
11 *fall'n* fallen (G)
15 *out* our (Ch, I, G)
16 *cut steel* crystal (Ch, G)

122 'SINGLY, TO POSSESS MY CHARMS' Source: HRO
Variants in Chawton, Isel and Gilson:
1 *Singly* Single (Ch)
2 *fearless* dauntless (Ch)
5 *toil* toils (Ch)
6 *gained* won (Ch) *me* [thee cancelled in I]
7 *But* Yet (Ch) *join'd with* joined to (Ch)
8 *my* a (G)
9 *my* our (G)
14 *when you've got us* when you find us

122 'SURE NEVER WAS CREATURE SO GROSSLY ABUSED' Source: HRO
Variants in Chawton, Isel, Gilson and Chute:
1 *Sure never was creature so grossly abused* Sure never was creature more
   grossly abused (Ch) Sure no one was ever so grossly abus'd (Chute)
2 *Of dullness more often or falsely accused* Of dullness so often and falsely
   accused (Chute)
3 *For men of my service regardless, still dare* For men, of my service unmindful,
   will dare (Ch) For men, of my service unmindful, still dare (Chute)
4 *thick headed blockhead* poor stupid Fellow (Ch) thick headed fellow (G)
5 *Yet* Tho' (Chute)
6 *happy* willing (Chute) *gain* get (Ch)
7 *To my mind or my manners* To my morals or manners (Ch) To my manner
   or morals (G) To my conduct or morals (Chute)
8 *I ne'er domineer* For I don't domineer (Chute)
9 *On each race course I'm seen, but no mortal ere yet* On each Race Course I'm
   found, but no one ever yet (Ch) I'm oft seen on a Race Course, tis true,
   but none yet (G) On each race course I'm seen, tho' no mortal e'er yet
   (Chute)
10 *ere* e'en (Ch) once (I, G, Chute)

144

11   *Though my heart's tough as oak* I've a heart tough as oak (Ch, Chute)
     yet (Ch, Chute) still (G)
13   *There is not much danger of my striking first* There is not much fear of my
     striking you first (Ch, Chute)
14   *But whoever attacks me will come off the worst* But if you attack me you will
     come off the worst (G)
15   *fault* thing (Chute) *I must own* I confess (Ch) *of true cowards a mark* of
     true coward a mark (G) of some cowards the mark (Chute)
16   *most* much (G)

123 'IF OUR COMPANY MAKES OUR TRUE CHARACTER KNOWN'
Source: HRO
Variants in Chawton, Isel and Gilson:
3   *I'm* since (G) *alledge* allege (I)
4   *gipsies* gypsies (Ch, I, G)
5   *dres't* dressed (Ch, I)
6   *cheerful* chearful (I) welcome (G)
8   *on* in(G)
10   *For though cheerful apart, we are dull when asunder* For though chearful
     together we're dull when asunder (Ch, I) For though cheerful together
     we are dull when asunder (G) [*apart in* HRO presumably copied in error
     from the line above]

123 'OF STRANGE & COMPOUND FORM AM I' Source: HRO
Variants in Chawton, Isel and Gilson:
2   *wav'd* waved (Ch, I, G)
8   *Anne* Ann (G)
9   *cleared* cleansed (Ch, G)

124 'PEG NICHOLSONS & SHERIFF KNIGHTS STAND BY' Source: Gilson.
Variants in HRO, Chawton and Isel:
1   *Knights* Knigths (HRO)
3   *confest* confess'd (HRO) confessed (I)
4   *drest* dress'd (HRO) dressed (I)
9   *show* shew (Ch)
10   *people* [omitted *in* HRO]

124 'DIVIDED, OF AN ANCIENT HOUSE AM I' Source: HRO
Variants in Chawton, Isel and Gilson:
Lines 1 and 3 indented in Gilson

125 'BY ALL PRUDENT FOLKS' Source: HRO
Variants in Chawton, Isel and Gilson:
4   *in sight* no right(Ch, I, G)

125 'IN MY FIRST, THAT HE MAY NOT BE TARDY OR LATE' Source: HRO
Variants in Chawton, Isel and Gilson:
No indentations in Gilson
1   *or* & (Ch, G, I)
6   *He should ever* He'll ever (Ch) That he'll ever (G)

125 'IF THERE BE TRUTH IN PROVERBS OLD' Source: HRO
Variants in Chawton, Isel, Gilson and Chute:
2   *Is best of servants, but of masters worst* Though best of servants is of masters
     worst (G) Is best of Servants & of Masters worst (Chute)
4   *Thus* There (Ch, I, Chute) Then (G) *triumph* victory (Ch, Chute)
5   *My whole a different sight more grateful gave* My whole, far different sight,
     & grateful gave (Ch) My whole a different scene more welcome gave
     (G) My whole, a different sight and grateful gave (G, I)
6   *Saw kings victorious, & a conquer'd knave* Saw Kings triumphant o'er a
     vanquished Knave (Ch) Saw Kings victorious o'er a conquer'd Knave
     (I) Saw Kings victorious & a vanquished Knave (G) Saw Kings
     triumphant, & a vanquish'd knave (Chute)
Below: Septr 1816 (Ch)

125 'MY FIRST A HORSEMAN'S DIRE DISGRACE WOULD TELL'
     Source: Chawton
Variants in Isel, Gilson and Chute:
2   *L* Ell (I, G, Chute)
4   *Will always* Would often (Chute)
6   *Can* Could (G)

126 'MY FIRST CAN WELL FINISH A BOTTLE OF WINE' Source: Gilson

126 MY 2^d MAY IN YOUTH BE VERY CHARMING' Source: Chawton
Variants in Isel:
2   *horribly* horridly

EXPLANATORY NOTES

1   AN EPISTLE TO FULWAR CRAVEN FOWLE ESQ[R].

Verse 'epistles' dedicated to a friend or acquaintance of the poet were written frequently in the eighteenth century; perhaps the best known is Pope's *Epistle to Dr. Arbuthnot*. The dedicatee of James Austen's poem was the 16 year-old son of the Revd Thomas Fowle, vicar of Kintbury, Berks (a place that had a special importance in James Austen's life and to which he refers in several poems) and brother of Tom, who became engaged to Cassandra Austen in 1792 but subsequently died of fever in the West Indies. The Fowle family were close friends and later relations by marriage of the Austens; Fulwar Craven had lived in Steventon rectory as one of Mr Austen's pupils and seems to have been a particular favourite of Mrs Austen. James wrote this poem the year after he had gone up to St John's College, Oxford, at the unusually early age of 14; Fulwar Craven was to matriculate a year later. In language at times more reminiscent perhaps of Milton's *Lycidas* than of Pope, James anticipates a time many years hence when he will urge Fulwar Craven, by now a great statesman, to look back on their youth, when they enjoyed simple country pleasures the year round. In fact they were both to follow the same calling, Fulwar Craven eventually succeeding his father to the incumbency of Kintbury in 1798 and remaining there until his death in 1840.

11   *Doric reed* Rustic, from the dialect of the Dorians in ancient Greece. Strictly speaking, a reed cannot be said to have an accent of any kind, representing as it does a musical instrument; but of course here it is a metaphor for the poem that James is writing, and we see what he means. Milton was more precise:

> Thus sang the uncouth swain to th' oaks and rills,
> While the still morn went out with sandals gray;
> He touched the tender stops of various quills,
> With eager thought warbling his Doric lay.
>   (*Lycidas*, 186-9)

James is possibly thinking also of the earlier line, 'Smooth-sliding Mincius, crowned with vocal reeds' (86).

24   *her lost mate bewails* The elegiac tone, while inappropriate to a poem supposedly dedicated to a living and famous man, is pardonable in a 15 year-old poet under the heady influence of English pastoral verse.

25   *Phœbus* The sun.

30   *Naïds* Water-nymphs.

37   *the dog-star's fiercer beams* Sirius, the dog-star, rises with the sun in July
      and was thought in the ancient world to add to its heat.
46   *Eurus* The east wind.

3   AN ELEGY – WRITTEN AT KINTBURY BERKS
Thomas Gray's *Elegy – Written in a Country Churchyard*, which appeared in
1751, is, as its name suggests, a poem commemorating the dead, specifically
'Th' unhonour'd Dead' who 'Along the cool sequester'd vale of life ... kept
the noiseless tenor of their way'; and it also provides an epitaph for the poet
who relates 'in these lines their artless tale'. James Austen, transposing his
Elegy from Stoke Poges to the Berkshire village of Kintbury, where his friend
Fulwar Craven Fowle's father was vicar *(see above)*, uses the term much more
loosely. The mood is elegiac, with 'The gothic Abbey's mould'ring ruins'
(always an architectural favourite with James) peeping through the 'solemn
gloom of night', while 'The night bird screams her melancholy song'. But the
'shadowy forms unnumbered... Noted by fancy's visionary eyes' are not the
objects of mourning — they merely contribute to the atmosphere of the poem;
and though the personifications of Contemplation and Solitude indicate the
poet's withdrawal from the world, it is only to amuse himself by thinking of
all those who, 'with pomp & glitter struck', delight 'To gain Ambition's frail
& tottering height / And stand conspicuous to the crowd below'. And instead
of Gray's concluding epitaph, James finishes with a compliment to the
conversational powers of his friend.
3   *Kennet's crystal stream* The river gives its name to the village (Kennet-
      bury).
7   *Cynthia's silver lamp* Cynthia was a poetic commonplace for the moon.
14   *a shell-framed grotto* James's verse moves from the topographical realism
      of the opening to an imaginary landscape of grottoes, ruined abbeys
      and deep cascades – an appropriately gothic setting for the 'shadowy
      forms' that inhabit it.
23   *The gothic Abbey's mould'ring ruins peep* Jane Austen was to mock her
      brother's taste for poetical gothic in her 'Ode to Pity', written when
      she was about 17:
           Ah! then what Lovely Scenes appear,
             The hut, the Cot, the Grot, & Chapel queer,
           And eke the Abbey too a mouldering heap,
             Conceal'd by aged pines her head doth rear
           And quite invisible doth take a peep.
      (See Jane Austen *Collected Poems and verse of the Austen family*, p.3.)
26   *the maddening crowd's tumultuous strife* cf. Gray's *Elegy*: 'Far from the
      madding crowd's ignoble strife' (73).

27   *gew-gaw* Bauble.
44   The change of metre in this line reads awkwardly; Pope's 'needless Alexandrine' comes to mind.
47   *Anacreon-like* Anacreon (6th cent. BC) wrote poetry celebrating wine, love and song.
      myrtle Sacred to Venus.
53   *farthest Scythia's trackless waste* Scythia was the ancient name for a large area of European and Asiatic Russia. In *King Lear* the people are invoked for their savage customs:

> The barbarous Scythian,
> Or he that makes his generation messes
> To gorge his appetite, shall to my bosom
> Be as well neighbour'd, pitied, and reliev'd
> As thou my sometime daughter.
>   (I.i. 1 16-20)

5   THE HERMIT

The Spenserian stanza in which this poem is written indicates the influence of *The Faerie Queene;* and indeed James Austen's 'ancient sage' with his 'silver hairs', living within 'the windings of a vaulted cell', recalls Spenser's 'aged Sire, in long blacke weedes yclad, / His feete all bare, his beard all hoarie gray' (Bk I, c.i, v.29) who conducts the Red Cross Knight and the virgin Una to his 'lowly Hermitage' (v.34). But whereas this hermit, who is in fact the enchanter Archimago, symbol of religious hypocrisy, lives 'Downe in a dale, hard by a forests side, / Far from resort of people', where he curses heaven and speaks 'reprochfull shame / Of highest God' (v.37), the one in James's poem is a sociable man who would 'with his friends the rural banquet share', who teaches the 'listening crowd' that 'happiness in virtue lies' and who throughout the seasons 'With grateful heart would frame the sacred lay / To him whose goodness great does all our pains o'er pay'.

1   *yon oak-crowned hill* James Austen places his hermit in a similar setting to the 'oak-crowned airy steep' from which the 'gothic Abbey's mould'ring ruins peep' in the *Elegy – written at Kintbury.*
6   *Maia's sweets* The sweet-scented flowers of May.
18   *the dull prosing sons of Pedantry & Pride* As the son of a clergyman (and destined to become one himself), James can hardly be attacking the clergy in general; his target is probably the Evangelicals. For a discussion of his attitude towards them, and his role in the SPCK, see Irene Collins, 'Too much zeal for the Bible Society: Jane Austen, her family, and the Religious Quarrels of her time' in the Jane Austen Society *Report* for 2001, pp.19-34.

25	*the Dog-star's parching ray* See note above, p. 148.

25   *the Dog-star's parching ray* See note above, p. 148.

55   *Thetis arms* The sea. 'Thetis fair' appears at the banquet of the sea gods in *The Faerie Queene,* Bk IV c.xi.

67   *Philomel all sad proclaims her wrong* Philomel was ravished by the Thracian king Tereus and was changed into a nightingale.

8   PROLOGUE TO THE TRAGEDY OF MATILDA

Dr Thomas Francklin's *Matilda* was the first of the series of plays to be produced by James Austen at Steventon rectory as family entertainments during the Christmas season. While later ones were comedies and burlesques, this was a sub-Jacobean tragedy in blank verse typical of the kind that abounded in the eighteenth century and which are today not even footnotes in theatrical histories. In fact, even this was not strictly a tragedy, since although it concerns murderous goings-on at the time of the Norrnan Conquest, it actually has a happy ending. In his Prologue, James gently mocks the affectations of the modern stage in contrast to the simple nature of earlier forms of drama.

1   *Thespis* Greek poet, supposedly the father of tragedy.

2   *his stage a cart* James Austen echoes the opening of Dryden's *Prologue at Oxford* (1684):

> *Thespis,* the first Professor of our Art,
> At Country Wakes sung Ballads from a Cart.

6   *Rosined lightening* Rosins or lacquers were used on silk or glass to give colour to stage lights.

7   *No iron bowl the rolling thunder forms* During the eighteenth century ingenious ways were found of creating stage effects. John Dennis invented the thunder roll for his *Appius and Virginia* (1709); the play was a failure and taken off but Dennis subsequently heard his device being used in a performance of *Macbeth* and protested, 'The villains will play my thunder but not my plays!'

9   *falchion* A curved sword

19   *tin* Property sword or dagger.

33   *the tragic lyre* The lyre was the stringed instrument of ancient Greece; here it stands for dramatic art.

35   *fondly* Dearly, but perhaps also with the older sense of foolishly.

9   EPILOGUE TO THE TRAGEDY OF MATILDA

The joke here is that the actors pretend to be surprised at the warm reception for their play; yet it is possible that James Austen's ironic description of *Matilda* as a 'dull tale' reflected his opinion of it. On the other hand, epilogues traditionally expressed a modest (and fictitious) apology for the play they followed, cf. Theseus to the mechanicals in *A Midsummer Night's Dream:* 'No epilogue, I pray you; for your play needs no excuse' (V.i. 363).

Mr T. *Fowle* Tom Fowle was still a pupil of Mr Austen's at the time of the performance in 1782.

4   *a vulgar Parson's pen* A less than respectful reference to Dr Francklin, the author, who was a clergyman.

7   *Olympian dew* A preparation for restoring the complexion of General Tracy, in Charlotte Smith's *The Old Manor House* (1794), who 'though he could not so totally baffle the inexorable hands of time as to escape a few wrinkles, he still maintained a considerable share of the bloom of youth, not without suspicion of Olympian dew, cold cream, and Spanish wool' (vol.II ch.1).

8   *cheapening* Haggling over prices with.

10   PROLOGUE TO THE RIVALS

Sheridan's comedy was first performed at Covent Garden in 1775 and was chosen by James Austen for a presentation at Steventon during his summer vacation from Oxford in 1784. Henry Austen, who spoke the Prologue, was thirteen; and clearly some other 'young Ladies and Gentleman' were invited to take part. In introducing a comedy, rather than the 'loftier numbers of the tragic Lyre', James expresses a purpose that his sister would later share: she too would 'paint 'the scene where wit & sense unite / To yield at once instruction & delight'.

19   *Ye blooming Fair* Jane and Cassandra would of course have been 'too young [their] stronger power to own', being respectively eleven and nine years old; but it is clear from the statement that when they are all older the men will be 'suppliants at [their] feet again' and 'they who liked as Boys shall love as men' that there must have been other girls in the audience.

11   EPILOGUE TO THE RIVALS

Written in the character of Bob Acres, and spoken by whoever took the role at Steventon, James Austen's Epilogue replaced Sheridan's original, which was given to the actress who played Julia and paid suitable tribute to the ladies ('"One moral's plain," cried I, "without more fuss; / Man's social happiness all rests on us'). Acres is the friend of Captain Absolute and, like him, is in love with Lydia Languish; he is unaware of his rival's identity, however, since Absolute is wooing her under the assumed name of Ensign Beverley. It is only when they meet to fight a duel arranged by Sir Lucius O'Trigger that he realises the truth.

2   *Odds tremors* In the play Acres has 'an odd kind of a new method of swearing' in which 'the oath should be an echo to the sense'; he calls it 'the *oath referential,* or *sentimental swearing',* and he regards it as very

'genteel'. Thus in the first scene in which he appears (II.i), he comments on the speed of his travelling with the oath 'Odds whips and wheels!' and we also have 'Odds blushes and blooms' (of Julia's health), 'odds minums and crotchets!' (of her harpsichord playing), 'odds swimmings' (of her dancing), 'odds frogs and tambours!', 'odds triggers and flints' – and so on throughout the play. He uses the expression 'odds tremors' before the duel (V.iii).

5   *Devonshire* Acres lives at Clod Hall, in Devonshire.

14   *his Counsellor* In drawing his sword, Sir Lucius says 'so come out, my little counsellor' (V. iii).

21   *Sir Lucius's plan* At the end of the play Sir Lucius generously arranges the various marriages: 'Come, now, I hope there is no dissatisfied person, but what is content; for as I have been disappointed myself, it will be very hard if I have not the satisfaction of seeing other people succeed better.' (V.iii)

11   THE RASH RESOLUTION

This is the earliest extant poem by James Austen that seeks to teach a lesson; when he grew older his own children – at least, James Edward and Caroline (see Introduction) – were to be on the receiving end of several, but here his pupil was his eleven year-old sister Cassandra, whose fault apparently was to vow one evening not to go to sleep until she had read the poem he was writing, only to find that she could not stay awake while he finished it. Even at the age of nineteen James was something of a moralist.

1   *Fair Eliza* There is no evidence that Cassandra (who was of course Cassandra Elizabeth) was ever called Eliza: she was known in the family as Cassy. In 'poeticising' her James uses a name that in its familiarity is more apt for verse than her other, more unusual one.

9   *A Youth of vacant head* A pleasantly self-deprecatory touch.

26   *the potent God* Morpheus.

29   *Betty* Possibly a real nursemaid at the rectory. At eleven, Cassandra must have been quite a weight to carry up to bed.

60   *the blessings of a Wife* The last verse is not a success: to conclude a light jest about a very small misdemeanour with the implication that unless Cassandra learns her lesson she may not find anyone to marry her is surely overdoing it.

14   SONNET TO LADY CATHERINE POWLET

In the seven sonnets by James Austen that have been preserved, the form, as was usual in the eighteenth century, is the Petrarchan as adopted by Milton, rather than the Shakespearean with its final rhyming couplet; James Austen preserves the usual shift in argument between the first eight lines and the last six. In the *Sonnet to Lady Catherine Powlet* the subject of the octave is the Hampshire landscape that James was often to describe in his poetry, and the language is characteristic of the proto-Romanticism of the period. In the sestet a classical setting is invoked only to be dismissed, since it is no longer haunted by the Queen of Love; she has now been subject to a metamorphosis and 'delights to rove' round the 'happier glades' of the ,Spring Wood in the form of a modern young lady. Lady Catherine Powlett was the daughter of the sixth Duke of Bolton, of Hackwood Park, near Basingstoke, and a cousin of the Revd Charles Powlett who tried to kiss Jane Austen (see *Letters*, p.4).

1   *Spring Wood* In 1725 the landscape gardener Charles Bridgeman laid out for the 3rd Duke of Bolton a spiked wheel pattern of rides in the Spring Wood at Hackwood Park. It can still be seen today.

9   *fair Idalic's love-devoted shades* The woods devoted to Venus (from Idalium in Cyprus, which was consecrated to the goddess).

10   *Paphos blooming grove* The line means much the same as the preceding one, Paphos being another city in ancient Cyprus dedicated to the worship of Venus.

14   SONNET TO WINTER

James Thomson published his long poem *The Seasons* in its complete (though not final) form in 1730 and it was immediately hugely popular; not only did it go into a large number of editions throughout the eighteenth century (and indeed subsequently), but it was translated into many languages, being especially favoured in Germany. Drawing on Virgil's *Georgics,* it examines the effects of Nature on human life, while at the same time demonstrating the suitability of landscape as a subject for poetry; thus it anticipated both the picturesque and Romanticism. James Austen, with his painter's eye and his love of the Hampshire countryside so familiar to him, could not fail to be affected by it and Thomson's influence can be clearly felt in these four sonnets, as well as in much of his later verse. *The Seasons* progresses from spring to winter, so that the poem is contained within the cycle of the year. The order of James's sonnets is not so clear, however; while in the Isel MS the sequence is the same as Thomson's, in Chawton it is winter, spring, autumn and summer. The latter may seem illogical, but the alexandrine with which summer finishes, highly unusual in a sonnet, suggests that he regarded it as the final line not just of the poem but of the sequence. In the *Sonnet to Winter,* the fierce assaults of the weather are tempered, in the sestet, by the pleasures of seasonable recreation.

1   *Stern Monarch of the howling tempests hail!* cf. the rhythm of the opening of *The Seasons:* 'Come, gentle Spring! ethereal Mildness! come ('Spring', 1).

2   *thy gloomy train* cf. *The Seasons:* 'Welcome, kindred glooms!' ('Winter', 5).

5   *cot* Cottage.

6   *rush-fringed brook* cf. Milton, *Comus*:

> By the rushy-fringèd bank,
> Where grows the willow and the osier dank ...
> (Sabrina's Song, 1-2)

distain Discolour, which is not good sense; 'distend' would have been better, had it fitted the rhyme scheme.

7   *chill frosts it's icy waves enchain* cf. *The Seasons*: 'The whole imprison'd river growls below' ('Winter', 727).

12   *bursts of mirth* The end of the sonnet reflects the winter pleasures described by Thomson:

> Rustic mirth goes round;
> The simple joke that takes the shepherd's heart,
> Easily pleas'd; the long loud laugh, sincere;
> The kiss, snatch'd hasty from the side-long maid,
> On purpose guardless, or pretending sleep:
> The leap, the slap, the haul; and, shook to notes
> Of native music, the resplendent dance.
> ('Winter', 617-23)

15   SONNET TO SPRING

Born in winter 'Gentle love' now begins to inspire 'pleasing pain'. Love is the theme of this sonnet and the spring is blessed for influencing the 'Fair one' in the poet's favour. In so far as the poem has a personal bearing, we may assume its subject to be Lady Catherine Powlett. 'Parent' and 'Youth' placed prominently in the first two lines may appear to be a slightly awkward contradiction; but both words contribute to the pervasive imagery of young love.

6   *the Idalian Boy* Cupid. His mother was Venus, hence 'Idalian' (see note to the *Sonnet to Lady Catherine Powlet*, page 153.

7   *His magic chains* Cupid's usual means of entrapping young maidens were his bow and arrow. This suggests Milton's enchanter Comus, who tells the virtuous Lady:

> if I but wave this wand,
> Your nerves are all chain'd up in alabaster...
> (*Comus*, ii. 1-2)

(The attendant Spirit later describes her as being 'In stony fetters fix'd'.)

12   *my ravish'd senses* The image of being held prisoner is transferred to the poet.

15   SONNET TO AUTUMN

The season is welcomed first for its attributes and then as an inspiration for the poet's verses, which of course are dedicated to his 'Fair one's praise'. In later life, James Austen was to write several poems about Autumn.

3   *Whether thou pleased survey'st the yellow plain* cf. *The Seasons:* 'Autumn, nodding o'er the yellow plain' ('Autumn', 2).

6   *mizzling* Raining lightly.

7   *Fane* Church.

16   SONNET TO SUMMER

This is the only sonnet in the sequence not to take love as a theme. Like the others, it begins with a personification of the season, though one of ambivalent gender, since the 'parted locks' could belong to a girl or a boy. The invocation of summer in the octave is complemented in the sestet by an explanation of its particular virtue, which is that its rains, intermixed with sunshine, will prepare country dwellers for the hardships of autumn and winter.

12   *distain* See note to the *Sonnet to Winter,* above. (It will be noticed that the the phrase 'torrent floods' is common to both lines.)

13   *submissive* Qualifies 'tenants', not 'smiles'.

16   SONNET ON LEAVING OXFORD

James Austen had been at Oxford for six years when he wrote this poem, coming down at the end of term in May 1785. A certain valedictory feel to it makes it possible that he was not intending to return for some time; and in the November of the following year he set off on a ten-month visit to the Continent. He was back in Oxford, however, by 1790, having taken his MA in 1788. The sonnet, following James's progress away from the realities of the city (and by extension the academic life) in the octave, leads him, in the sestet, into a world of fancy and imagination, where the moonlight directs his 'dubious way'. The opening description is reminiscent of a sonnet by James's contemporary at Oxford, Thomas Russell (1762-1788); this however was only published posthumously in 1789:

Sonnet

To Oxford

Oxford, since late I left thy peaceful shore,
Much I regret thy domes with turrets crown'd,
Thy crested walls with twining ivy bound,
Thy Gothic fanes, dim isles, and cloysters hoar,
And treasur'd rolls of Wisdom's ancient lore;
Nor less thy varying bells, which hourly sound
In pensive chime, or ring in lively round,
Or toll in the slow Curfeu's solemn roar;
Much too thy moonlight walks, and musings grave
Mid silent shades of high-embowering trees,

And much thy Sister-Streams, whose willows wave
In whispering cadence to the evening breeze;
But most those Friends, whose much-lov'd converse gave
Thy gentle charms a tenfold power to please.
                        (Sonnets and Miscellaneous Poems)

Perhaps James Austen was one of those friends.

4   *the far seen hill* Probably Boar's Hill, south of Oxford, which the Newbury road passes.

14   *radiance pale* The reversal of adjective and noun betrays the influence of Milton.

17   LINES ADDRESSED TO MISS CHARLOTTE BRYDGES

A love poem couched in somewhat conventional language, though the final image of a ship's pilot unable to guide his vessel between two rocks is quite striking. Charlotte Brydges was a younger sister of Madam Lefroy, Jane Austen's friend and mentor; she and her brother Egerton spent two years at Deane parsonage, which they rented from Mr Austen, in order to be near the Lefroys in the neighbouring parish of Ashe. Charlotte subsequently was married twice, on neither occasion to James Austen.

6   The blank of course stands for 'Charlotte's'.

17   SONNET TO THE SAME

The theme of this sonnet is the instruction of the poet by the young lady to whom it is addressed (i.e. Charlotte Brydges); if it is too much to ask her to tell him what words to speak or what acts to perform to gain her favour, she must teach him how to die.

1   *whose opening charms... own* The sense is 'whose budding charms, which are as fair as morning, are acknowledged by numberless silently sorrowing hearts'.

4   *in measure meet* In appropriate verse.

18   PROLOGUE TO THE WONDER

When James Austen returned from the Continent in the autumn of 1787, the Christmas theatricals at Steventon could begin again. He had originally intended to produce two plays, *Which is the Man?* and *Bon Ton*, but eventually the choice was Mrs Centlivre's comedy of 1714, *The Wonder – a Woman keeps a secret!*, and a week or so later *The Chances*, an adaptation by Garrick of Fletcher's original text. This was the first occasion on which the Austens' lively cousin Eliza de Feuillide took part; in *The Wonder* she would have played the heroine, Violante, who keeps secret the hiding place of her friend Isabella until she can defeat the plans for a forced marriage to a man she does not love and marry the man she does. Garrick had so liked the leading role in *The Wonder* that he played it more than 65 times during his last 20 years on the stage, and it was his final part before retiring in 1776. James's prologue does not refer to the play but rather to the history of the Christmas celebrations during which it was to be presented.

21   *Imported from... France* Names of sixteenth-century court dances – basse danse, haute danse, galliard branle, tourdion or cinq-pace – point to their origin in France.

22   *with awkward steps* James conjures up a vision of sturdy English yeomen pluckily doing their best to get their feet round fancy French steps, but there is no reason to suppose that Elizabeth's courtiers were not just as accomplished in dancing as their French counterparts.

25   *Leicester* A painting at Penshurst Place in Kent purportedly shows the Earl of Leicester dancing La Volta with the Queen.

27   *Distinguished both by ugliness & dress* A sideswipe at Elizabeth that would have delighted the twelve year-old Jane, who detested her because she had had Mary Queen of Scots executed.

31   *a set of men* The Puritans.

33   *Rebrobation* A misspelling of reprobation, which in Calvinist doctrine means rejection by God.

40   *Charles* Charles II.

20   EPILOGUE TO THE COMEDY OF THE WONDER

A light-hearted contribution to the debate about the role and position of women, the poem presents the eighteenth century, when 'learning's sacred light / Rose to disperse the shades of Gothic night', as the period in which women were finally able to force men to submit to their 'superior rule'; and Mrs Centlivre, the 'night's gay authoress', is cited as the champion of the 'female cause'.

Appropriately the epilogue is given to the heroine of the play.

11   *the listed field* I.e. lists, the enclosed space where in the Middle Ages tournaments were held.

23   *usurpation* Suggesting that male domination of women was not the original state of things.

31   *myrtle* Sacred to Venus, and therefore an emblem of love.
        wreath of bays Bay wreaths were accorded by the Romans to victorious generals.

41   James Austen concludes his epilogue with an alexandrine. (See note to *An Elegy – written at Kintbury* above, p.149.)

21   PROLOGUE TO THE CHANCES

In what was perhaps his most accomplished poem to date, James Austen satirises one of the great occupations of his century, gaming. If the sustained irony of the opening is a little obvious, it is more than compensated for by the deftness with which he deploys a series of gambling metaphors at the end. The title refers to throws at dice or cards. Other plays had been written with titles derived from games, including Middleton's *A Game at Chess* (1624), Mrs Centlivre's *The Basset Table* (I 705) and no fewer than three called *The Gamester* (by Shirley, 1633, Mrs Centlivre, 1705 and Edward Moore, 1753). *The Chances* was adapted by Garrick from Fletcher's original of 1647, which itself had been adapted from a novel by Cervantes.

22   *"Such things were"* 'I cannot but remember such things were, / That were most precious to me' *(Macbeth,* IV.iii. 222-3).

39   *of one* I.e. of one score (20).

42   *play* Gambling.

46   *at Winchester or Eton* Like his brothers, James Austen received his schooling at home from his father; however he was to send his own son, James Edward, to Winchester College having, interestingly enough, originally intended him for Eton.

48   *E & O* E O was a game of chance in which the ball went into one of a number of niches marked with either an E or an O.

53   *"Pay whom you must... man"* James conflates two couplets from Pope's *Essay on Man*:

> Laugh where we must, be candid where we can;
> But vindicate the ways of God to Man.
> (Epistle I 15-16)
> Know then thyself, presume not God to scan;
> The proper study of Mankind is Man.
> (Epistle II 1-2)

56   *Lilly's grammar Rules of Latin Syntax by* William Lily ('Lily the Grammarian') was printed in 1529, but James Austen would probably have known it from a later edition such as that of 1680, published as *A Short Introduction of Grammar. Compiled and set forth for the bringing up of all those that attain to the knowledge of the Latin tongue.*
the chances Calculation of the likelihood of throws in dice or cards.

57   *Hoyle* Edmond Hoyle's *The Accurate Gamester's Companion* was published in 1745. *Mr Hoyle's Games* went through many editions in the eighteenth century. Subsequently the name Hoyle became synonymous with rules for indoor games.
Paine William Payne, *Maxims for Playing the Game of Whist etc,* 1773.

58   *all fours* A tavern game dating from the seventeenth century, its name deriving from the four points available, High, Low, Jack and Game. Generally popular with the lower classes, it was the game which first used the term 'jack' for knave.

68   *die* Singular of dice.

23   PROLOGUE TO THE TRAGEDY OF TOM THUMB
Fielding's *Tom Thumb* was anything but a tragedy. First performed at the
Haymarket in 1730, when its author was only 23, it was a blank verse burlesque
in which the conquering hero was the dwarf of the title. The play was set in
an absurd kind of Arthurian court and included a satirical attack on Sir Robert
Walpole; it was a great success and in a revised version in 1731, under the
title *The Tragedy of Tragedies*, it played for nearly 40 nights – a long run at that
time. In the prologue, James Austen reflects his recent travels in a survey of
continental pastimes, before settling down to describe pleasures closer to
home.

10   *pleasure reigns man's great concern alone* James here is speaking lightly,
        as he reveals two lines later in the phrase 'killing time'; yet since his
        concern is with social, rather than individual, pleasures, he may be
        reflecting something of Pope's view in the *Essay on Man* that God 'makes
        what Happiness we justly call / Subsist not in the good of one, but all'
        (Epistle IV 37-8).

22   *Farmers general* One of the abuses of the Ancien Régime was the farming
        of indirect taxes by those who had paid a fixed sum for the lease on a
        six-year contract and who enriched themselves on the profits.

26   *catgut* Used for violin strings.

32   *the capital of fall'n Navarre* Pamplona, where the running of the bulls
        takes place in July.

33   *Dressed for the fight* Bullfights are held at this time.

41   *Holland* James's ungenerous portrayal of the Dutch is typical of its
        period; since the Anglo-Dutch wars of the 17th century, they had been
        characterised as stupid, unimaginative and drunken.

50   *December's skies* The depiction of skaters seems to be a caricature of a
        winter scene of the Dutch School.

67   *the striker's motion watch* Striker was perhaps the more usual term for
        batsman. Charles Powlett of Hackwood Park was the driving force
        behind the Hambledon Cricket Club, which, two years before James
        wrote the poem, had won a famous match against the men of Kent. For
        the Austens' connections with the game, see Michael Davis, 'Jane Austen
        and Cricket', in the Jane Austen Society *Report* for 2000.

87   *Oft with our partner's blunders find great fault* As Mrs Norris and Dr Grant
        are given to doing (see *Mansfield Park* vol.II ch. 7).

114   *Philip's son* Alexander the Great (the son of Philip of Macedon).

115   *him* I.e. James himself.

As this is the only one of James Austen's prologues and epilogues not to name the play it accompanied, it is possible that on this occasion the dramatist was James himself. One of Jane's playlets in *Volume the First*, 'The Visit', which was probably written in 1789, is dedicated to him; the 14 year-old authoress modestly proclaims that her drama is 'inferior to those celebrated Comedies called "The School for Jealousy" & "The travelled Man"' (*Minor Works* p.49). Since there is no record of plays with any such titles being published or performed professionally, it is possible that these were his own works presented the year before (Salieri's opera *La Scola de' Gelosi* had been given in London in March 1786, and the first of these plays may have been adapted from its libretto). In the prologue James takes Shakespeare's 'All the world's a stage' as his starting point and satirically examines the various forms of insincerity in public and private life.

1   *the Bard* Shakespeare, in *As You Like It*, II.vii. 139-40.

8   *And each one in his time plays many parts* cf. *As You Like It*, ll.vii. 143: 'And one man in his time plays many parts'.

30   *the uncourteous retort* James is again thinking of *As You Like It*:
O sir, we quarrel in print, by the book; as you have books for good manners. I will name you the degrees. The first, the Retort Courteous; the second, the Quip Modest; the third, the Reply Churlish; the fourth, the Reproof Valiant; the fifth, the Countercheck Quarrelsome; the sixth, the Lie with Circumstance; the seventh, the Lie Direct. (V.iv. 89-96.)

32   *Hotspur... the Devil of Glendower* In *Henry IV Part I* Falstaff refers to 'that fiend Douglas, that spirit Percy, and that devil Glendower' (II.iv. 364-5).

48   *India Bonds* Bonds issued by the East India Company.

27   EPILOGUE TO THE SULTAN

In *The Sultan* by Isaac Bickerstaffe (1775) the heroine, a lively English girl, Roxalana, sees off the entire harem and becomes sole empress. The tactics that she practises so persuasively on the Sultan are here given a domestic setting. Although the dialogue does not take place at bedtime, it resembles a curtain lecture, as the phrase 'behind the connubial curtain' perhaps suggests. In fact it in many ways anticipates Douglas Jerrold's *Mrs Caudle's Curtain Lectures*, which appeared in *Punch* in 1845 (Jerrold was a midshipman in Charles Austen's ship the *Namur* anchored at the Nore in 1813, and 'recalled that he owed his start to Captain Austen, "a relative of the novelist", when he became well known as a humorist) (Park Honan, *Jane Austen: Her Life*, p.332); since there were both a library and a theatre on board, it is quite possible that he knew of James Austen's prologues and epilogues. The epilogue was spoken by Jane Cooper, daughter of Mrs Austen's sister.

22   *the Club* A periodic meeting of, in Johnson's phrase, 'good fellows' at a

tavern. Mrs Caudle's opinions of her husband's joining such a club, 'the Skylarks', are the subject of the third *Curtain Lecture*.

33   *her Husband who teazes* Who persistently vexes her husband.

51   *Divan* The Turkish council of state presided over by the sultan; hence, here, the audience.

29   THE MAID OF THE MOOR

Not included in any of the three albums of James Austen's verses, this poem exists only in an unidentified hand on a sheet of paper with the watermark 1802. Assuming it was written close to this date, it could have been intended to amuse his daughter Anna, who in that year was 9 years old. On the other hand, it may date from an earlier period and have been written for one of his younger brothers or sisters. Its humorous and punning style is not like any of his other known verse, but the Shakespeare quotations are characteristic of him.

2   *the heath frequenting grouse* There speaks a sportsman: in his younger years at least James held a game duty certificate.

5   *with lips of glue* A curious expression, probably merely intended to be comically inappropriate. There was however a substance known as 'lip-glue', which was a combination of glue and sugar and was moistened by the tongue.

11   *barbed steeds, – from the Bull's head* The juxtaposition of the romantic and the mundane sets the tone for the comedy of the poem.

15   *two small rattling bits of bone* Dice.

19   *unseen must blush in wintry snows* cf. Gray's *Elegy – Written in a Country Churchyard*: 'Full many a flower is born to blush unseen' (55).

55   *hot-beds* Beds of earth heated by fermenting manure, thus both appropriate and inappropriate here.

60   *to rake* To be a rake, to lead a dissolute life.

74   *Flesh ... is Grass* 'All flesh is grass, and all the goodliness thereof is as the flower of the field' (Isaiah xl 6).

92   *a mole of four to th'pound* A large piece of which four would weigh a pound.

95   *a Coffin* I.e. a spark whose shape suggested a coffin.

97   *Spiders their busy death watch tick'd* Several kinds of insects, not just beetles, were said to tick like a watch, the sound supposedly portending death.

109 *And "o'er the one half-world, seem'd dead:"* Cf. *Macbeth*:

Now o'er the one half-world
Nature seems dead, and wicked dreams abuse
The curtain'd sleep...   (II.i. 49-51)

118 *Green, green his waistcoat was, as leeks* cf. *A Midsummer Night's Dream*:

'His eyes were green as leeks' (V.i. 343).

129 *Four fathoms deep thy love doth lye* cf. Ariel's song in *The Tempest*: 'Full fathom five thy father lies' (I.ii. 394).

136 "Bow Wow"! James may have been thinking of the song that immediately precedes 'Full fathom five': 'Come unto these yellow sands' has the refrain:

> Hark, hark!
>> Bow, wow,
> The watch-dogs bark:
>> Bow, wow,
> Hark, hark! I hear
> The strain of strutting Chanticleer
>> Cry, Cock-a-diddle-dow.
> *(The Tempest*, I.ii.375-84)

138 *holland* A linen fabric.

144 *souse* Plunge.

145 *the fair* The woman.

148 the bottom of a Well The Proverb comes from Diogenes Laertius: We know nothing certain; for truth is hidden at the bottom of a well.

33   APRIL. 1805 TO MARY

Though not descibed as such, this is an ode. Whilst it makes use of the kind of stanza form that James Austen might have found in the odes of Gray or Collins, it lacks the variety of structure and length demonstrated in their works and the stanzas are all of the same pattern, except for one possibly accidental irregularity. The dedication is to his second wife, Mary, though the poem is actually addressed to the month of April and it is only at the end that its particular significance for him, that it contains her birthday, is revealed. That he should 'love... April most' because it brought her 'natal day' may perhaps seem a little obsessive; a fortnight before he wrote it, however, her mother had died, and it may be that the tenderness of expression in the poem was intended as a consolation.

25 *After long absence of a year* The retrospective tone of this stanza anticipates in a general way the particular anniversary celebrated at the end of the poem.

30 *And bids us live our past lives o'er again.* It is possible that at the midway point of the poem, when the past is about to give way to thoughts of the future, James Austen deliberately substitutes a pentameter for the expected alexandrine; it may equally have been an oversight.

34 *Haply's* Is perhaps.

45 *joy and pleasure ... alternate reign* cf. Blake's 'Auguries of Innocence' (written c.1801-3 but unpublished in Blake's lifetime):

Man was made for joy and woe;
And when this we rightly know,
Thro' the world we safely go.
Joy and woe are woven fine,
A clothing for the soul divine;
Under every grief and pine
Runs a joy with silken twine.   (56-62)

52 *her natal day* Mary Lloyd was born on 17 April 1771.
55 *eight revolving years* James and Mary were married on 17 January 1797.

35   TO EDWARD ON THE DEATH OF HIS FIRST PONY
In what is perhaps the most touching of all his verses, James Austen consoles
the 12 year-old Edward (his 'weeping boy') with the idea that the loss of the
pony offers an opportunity to prepare his mind for the 'more serious ills of
life'. Yet 'reason' teaches that only those ills 'which on ourselves we bring'
can truly make us suffer, and 'every sorrow will be light, / When all within
our breasts is right'. Whilst there is something of the sermon here, it is precisely
the same sentiment that Colonel Brandon expresses about Marianne's betrayal
by Willoughby: 'She will feel her own sufferings to be nothing. They proceed
from no misconduct, and can bring no disgrace' *(Sense and Sensibility*, p.210).
S&S was published later the same year (1811).
2   *Pony dead* Mary Lloyd, James Austen's wife, noted in her pocket-book
        for 30 January 1811, 'Edward's pony died suddenly'. In her
        Reminiscences Caroline, who was five at the time, gives an account of
        the sad event: 'I saw its dying struggles in the stable, having been taken
        out there by one of the maids, who hurried me off again directly. This
        was a great grief to my brother, and some to me. Pony was sorrowfully
        interred in a corner of the Home Meadow, and his grave was discernible
        for some years afterwards.' (25) Six months later the pony was replaced
        by another, called Sutton, which Edward rode to hounds.
12   *saintefoin* A low-growing forage plant.
17   *sieve* A basket used for market produce, here no doubt holding fodder.
34   *corse* Corpse.
38   *His Father's hand in silence took* This touchingly observed action is used
        as a fulcrum between the two long passages of speech.

37   TO CAROLINE – ON HER BIRTHDAY
Caroline Mary Craven Austen was born at Steventon on 18 June 1805. She
was thus, as her father says, six years old when this poem was written for her,
which may seem rather young to be the recipient of quite such insistent moral
and religious exhortations. But at this time James Austen was undertaking

his duties with considerable energy: two years later he was to set up a District Committee of the SPCK for the Deaneries of Basingstoke and Alton (see Irene Collins, 'Too much zeal for the Bible Society: Jane Austen, her family, and the Religious Quarrels of her time', Jane Austen Society *Report* for 2001) The banishment, at the opening, of the Muses as 'beings which have no existence' sets the tone for a poem that urges Caroline to pray to that Power 'by whom our good / And evil, best are understood' for help should she ever be tempted to be led astray by fashion and become a selfish and vain 'modern Miss', thereby causing her family to keep her birthday 'with less joy'. The 'sorrowing look' with which the child greets these cheerful sentiments speaks for itself.

2   *you fictitious Nine* The Muses. James Austen rejects the traditional appeal to the poetic muse for inspiration.

7   *gives just offence* It did not do so to Milton, although admittedly he adapted the Greek original to suit a Christian sensibility:

> Of Man's first disobedience and the fruit
> Of that forbidden tree, whose mortal taste
> Brought death into the world and all our woe,
> With loss of Eden, till one greater Man
> Restore us and regain the blissful seat,
> Sing heav'nly Muse, that on the secret top
> Of Oreb, or of Sinai, didst inspire
> That shepherd, who first taught the chosen seed,
> In the beginning how the heav'ns and earth
> Rose out of Chaos...   (*Paradise Lost* Bk I 1-10)

In *Lycidas* Milton is happy frankly to invoke the 'Sisters of the sacred well' (15).

12   *his favourite's praise* Though James Austen wrote poems for Caroline and James Edward, he is not known ever to have done so for Anna.

54   *friends* Family.

65   *on Samuel's young but pious head* See I *Samuel* III. i-xviii.

39   TO MISS JANE AUSTEN THE REPUTED AUTHOR OF SENSE AND SENSIBILITY

For attribution to James Austen, see textual note.

1   *On such Subjects* I.e. sense and sensibility.

3   *Sterne's darling Maid* Sterne, *A Sentimental Journey*: '– Dear sensibility! source inexhausted of all that's precious in our joys, or costly in our sorrows!' (vol.2, 'The Bourbonnois').

Fair Elinor's Self In *Sense and Sensibility* Elinor Dashwood embodies the quality of sense and her sister Marianne that of undisciplined feeling.

39   TO MARY, ON HER WEDDING DAY

James Austen and Mary Lloyd were married at Hurstbourne Tarrant, near Andover, Hampshire, the parish church for the Lloyds' home at Ibthorpe, on 17 January 1797. The cold winter's day, with the sun brightening the cold snowy landscape, gives James his metaphor for their marriage: life's ills would be made tolerable to him by her love. This is a remarkable testimony to the warmth of James's feelings for his wife and, at least in regard to himself, justifes his mother's assertion in welcoming her new daughter-in-law into the family fifteen years before that she would 'greatly increase & promote the happiness' of James, Anna and herself. Jane, by the time this poem was written, appears to have felt somewhat differently.

34   *The invalid's severest trial* In middle age, James had lost much of his earlier cheerfulness and had become rather restless and melancholy. Jane wrote to Cassandra in February 1807, when he had been visiting them in Southampton: 'I am sorry & angry that his Visits should not give one more pleasure; the company of so good & so clever a Man ought to be gratifying in itself:—but his Chat seems all forced, his Opinions on many points too much copied from his Wife's, & his time here is spent I think in walking about the House & banging the Doors, or ringing the Bell for a glass of Water.' *(Letters*, p.121)

44   *temper mild* When Jane Austen made the journey from Chawton to Winchester in her final illness, James's carriage was sent over from Steventon especially to take her. 'Now that's a sort of thing,' she wrote to her friend Anne Sharp, 'which Mrs J. Austen does in the kindest manner! – But still she is in the main *not* a liberal-minded Woman...' *(Letters*, pp340-41).

56   *the "last, best gift of Heaven"* In *Paradise Lost* Adam calls Eve 'Heav'n's last best gift' (Bk.V 19).

41   LINES WRITTEN AT KINTBURY — MAY 1812

Beginning with an evocation of youthful visits to the Fowle family at Kintbury, inspired by revisiting the village on a bright May day, James Austen writes an elegy for Tom, who died in the West Indies in February 1797, having five years earlier become engaged to Cassandra. This is an uneven poem: the picture of domestic hospitality, though couched in somewhat self-consciously literary language, is touching; less convincing perhaps is the concluding eulogy to Mary, in which James returns to the sentiments, and even the phraseology, of his previous tribute to her.

10   *Mansion white* The reflected group of church, tree and mansion is a charming way of introducing the vicarage, home between 1741 and 1840 to three generations of the Fowle family. It was subsequently

demolished and replaced by the present Victorian building, now a private house.

59   *The Father grave* In January 1796 Jane wrote to Cassandra, who was staying at Kinthury to be with Tom Fowle before his departure for the West Indies: 'I am very glad to find from Mary that Mr & Mrs Fowle are pleased with you. I hope you will continue to give satisfaction.' (*Letters*, p.4) This may of course merely indicate officiousness on the part of Mary Lloyd, but it is possiblJy indicative of a certain stiffness in the Fowles (and of Jane's characteristic reaction).

63   *on hospitable thoughts intent* cf. *Paradise Lost:*

> with dispatchful looks in haste
> She turnș, on hospitable thoughts intent
> What choice to choose for delicacy best,
> What order, so contrived as not to mix
> Tastes not well joined, inelegant, but bring
> Taste after taste upheld with kindliest change...
>
> (Bk.V. 331-6)

67   *four manly boys* Fulwar Craven, Tom, William and Charles Fowle.

74   *close by the path their feet have often trod* Both Mr Fowle and his fourth son, Charles, died at Kintbury in February 1806 and were buried there on the same day (17 February).

75   *sedgy Nile* William Fowle was a physician with the army and died in Egypt in 1801.

78   *'gainst western India's shores* Tom Fowle died of fever at San Domingo in 1797.

91   *a dearer tie* Tom and Cassandra had become engaged, probably in 1792.

95   *So man proposes* Cf. 'Man proposes but God disposes' (originally in the *Imitatio Christi*).

106   *when first beneath this roof we met* Mary Lloyd was first cousin to the Fowle brothers, her mother being the sister of Mrs Fowle. Her sister Eliza married Fulwar Craven in 1788 and in the following year the Lloyd family rented Deane parsonage from Mr Austen. James had therefore known Mary well before he married Anne Mathew in 1792; and in the following lines he writes of her as if that marriage had not supervened.

116   *this artless Lay* This is a favourite phrase of James Austen's. cf. *To Mary, on her Wedding Day*, 57.

44   HOME

James sometimes took his family to visit his friend the Revd Fulwar Craven Fowle, who succeeded his father as vicar of Kintbury in 1798: Caroline wrote of the year 1812 'We went several times to stay – we were at Kintbury, Speen and Chawton' (*Reminiscences*, p.27). On this occasion, however, he went alone, and the theme of the poem is the particular attraction that his own village of Steventon has for him, in that not only was it the scene of his 'early hopes & fears', but now it is where his 'little flock secure is laid' and of course where he receives 'Such welcome sweet as love can give / From those, whom each revolving year, / Renders more valued & more dear'. As so often, his description of the country he passes through on his homeward journey is couched in the language of the artist; and there is a characteristic sense of history in the reference to 'The warlike chiefs of former years'.

18 *"my own, my native land"* cf. Scott, *The Lay of the Last Minstrel:*

  Breathes there the man, with soul so dead,
  Who never to himself hath said,
   This is my own, my native land!
  Whose heart hath ne'er within him burn'd,
  As home his footsteps he hath turn'd
   From wandering on a foreign strand! (Canto vi v.i)

19 *Highelere's varied ground* Highclere, Hampshire was the site of a medieval castle belonging to the bishops of Winchester. The house of James Austen's day was completely rebuilt, 1839-40, for the 3rd Earl of Carnarvon by Sir Charles Barry, architect of the Houses of Parliament.

44 *bents* Reed-like grass with stiff, rigid stems.

57 *the village small* James Edward wrote in the *Memoir:* 'Of this somewhat tame country, Steventon, from the fall of the ground, and the abundance of its timber, is certainly one of the prettiest spots' (ch. 2).

46 SELBOURNE HANGER

The village of Selborne, $3^1/2$ miles south-east of Chawton, was the home of the naturalist Gilbert White, to whom James Austen pays tribute in this poem. The opening 49 lines provide one of the most sustained passages of artistic landscape description in James's poetry. Indeed, it might almost be said to constitute a drawing lesson: the spectator is invited to take as much care in observing the scene as if he were to depict it on paper. From its fixed vantage point the reader's eye follows the poet's over 'the landscape's wild variety' as if it were looking at a picture rather than reading a poem; and pictorial imagery is so deeply ingrained in the verse that poet and reader – and even at one point nature herself – appear to be engaged in drawing the scene. As in other poems about the Hampshire country that James knew so well, a sense of history, indeed of romance, is conveyed through the evocation of monks in an old abbey, of wandering pilgrims, knights and barons. The seclusion of 'natures scenery lone and wild' affords an opportunity to reflect that true happiness lies in the 'well cultivated mind' found in 'nature's true heirs'; but such abstract speculation gives way to a much more specific contemplation of natural history in Gilbert White's book.

1   *Selbourne Hanger* 'The high part of the south-west consists of a vast hill of chalk, rising three hundred feet above the village, and is divided into a sheep-down, the high wood and a long hanging wood, called The Hanger. The covert of this eminence is altogether beech, the most lovely of all forest trees, whether we consider its smooth rind or bark, its glossy foliage, or graceful pendulous boughs. The down, or sheepwalk, is a pleasing park-like spot, of about one mile by half that space, jutting out on the verge of the hill-country, where it begins to break down into the plains, and commanding a very engaging view, being an assemblage of hill, dale, woodlands, heath, and water. The prospect is bounded to the south-east and east by the vast range of mountains called the Sussex Downs, by Guild-down near Guildford, and by the Downs round Dorking, and Ryegate in Surrey, to the north-east, which altogether, with the country beyond Alton and Farnham, form a noble and extensive outline.' (Gilbert White, *The Natural History of Selborne*, Letters to Thomas Pennant, I)

27   *the wooded hill of Nore* 'A noble chalk promontory, remarkable for sending forth two streams [the Arun and the Wey] into two different seas'(*The Natural History of Selborne*, Letters to Thomas Pennant, I). James's eye moves south-easterly over the view.

30   *Frensham* Rather further away, across the border in Surrey.

32   *Wolmer* 'The royal forest of Wolmer is a tract of land of about seven miles in length, by two and a-half in breadth, running nearly from north to south....This royalty consists entirely of sand covered with heath and fern; but is somewhat diversified with hills and dales, without having one standing tree in the whole extent.' (*The Natural History of Selborne:* Letters to Thomas Pennant, VI)

35   *the dark heath's monotony* Wolmer Forest might however have appealed to James's sporting tastes, since Gilbert White wrote that it was a 'very agreeable haunt for many sorts of wild fowls' and that it had often afforded him 'much entertainment both as a sportsman and as a naturalist' (*The Natural History of Selborne*, Letters to Thomas Pennant, VI).

42   *the Zigzag walk* Constructed by Gilbert White and his brother John in 1752 and 1753.

47   *the village* 'At the foot of this hill, one stage or step from the uplands, lies the village, which consists of one single straggling street, three-quarters of a mile in length, in a sheltered vale, and running parallel with The Hanger.' (*The Natural History of Selborne*, ' Letters to Thomas Pennant, I)

54   *the fallen Priory* The ruins of a priory founded by Peter de Rupibus, Bishop of Winchester, referred to by Gilbert White in his poem 'The Invitation to Selborne':

Adown the vale, in lone, sequester'd nook,
Where skirting woods imbrown the dimpling brook,
The ruin'd Convent lies; here wont to dwell
The lazy canon midst his cloister'd cell;
While papal darkness brooded o'er the land,
Ere Reformation made her glorious stand:
Still oft at eve belated shepherd-swains
See the cowl'd spectre skim the folded plains. (45-52)

59   *tall pillars massy proof* cf. Milton, *Il Penseroso*:

But let my due feet never fail
To walk the studious cloister's pale,
And love the high embowèd roof,
With antique pillars massy proof...   (155-8)

64   *vain hope* James reflects a similar view of Roman Catholic rites to that
of Gilbert White, though he is perhaps a little more charitable to the
monks who practised them.

154   *And does not think of Gilbert White? The Natural History of Selborne* appeals
to James for its scientific enquiry into the flora and fauna of the village;
but he also presumably knew White's poem 'Selborne Hanger', written
in November 1763, which however is very different from his own, since
it describes the scene in winter, when it is a 'savage landscape, bleak
and bare' (21).

172   *the Reed-sparrows tiny throat* The lesser reed-sparrow, or sedge-bird, is
described by White as singing 'incessantly night and day during the
breeding-time, imitating the note of a sparrow, a swallow, a skylark'
and as having 'a strange, hurrying manner in its song' (*The Natural
History of Selborne*, Letters to Thomas Pennant, XXV).

173   *Descend the Chimney's shaft*

... in general with us this *hirundo* breeds in chimneys, and
loves to haunt those stacks where there is a constant fire, no
doubt for the sake of warmth. Not that it can subsist in the
immediate shaft where there is a fire, but prefers one
adjoining to that of the kitchen, and disregards the perpetual
smoke of that funnel, as I have often observed with some
degree of wonder.

Five or six or more feet down the chimney does this little
bird begin to form her nest about the middle of May, which
consists, like that of the house-martin, of a crust or shell
composed of dirt or mud, mixed with short pieces of straw
to render it tough and permanent; with this difference, that
whereas the shell of the martin is nearly hemispheric, that of
the swallow is open at the top, and like half a deep dish.

169

This nest is lined with fine grasses and feathers, which are often collected as they float in the air....

The swallow lays from four to six white eggs, dotted with red specks; and brings out her first brood about the last week in June, or the first week in July. (*The Natural History of Selborne,* Letters to the Hon. Daines Barrington, XVIII)

175   *the old Tortoise* 'A land tortoise, which has been kept for thirty years in a little walled court belonging to the house where I now am visiting, retires under ground about the middle of November, and comes forth again about the middle of April. When it first appears in the spring it discovers very little inclination towards food; but in the height of summer grows voracious; and then as the summer declines its appetite declines; so that for the last six weeks in autumn it hardly eats at all. Milky plants, such as lettuces, dandelions, sowthistles, are its favourite dish. In a neighbouring village one was kept till by tradition it was supposed to be a hundred years old. An instance of vast longevity in such a poor reptile!' (*The Natural History [of Selborne,* Letters to the Hon. Daines Barrington, Letter VII) 'The old tortoise, that I have mentioned in a former letter, still continues in this garden, and retired underground about the 20th November, and came out again for one day on the 30th: it lies now buried in a wet swampy border under a wall facing to the south, and is enveloped at present in mud and mire!' (Letter XVII)

188   *Grongar Hill* Grongar Hill, near Llandeilo, Carmarthenshire, was the subject of a popular poem by John Dyer, first published in 1726, that in both its rhythm and its themes was clearly influential on James's poem. The landscape is portrayed in terms of visual art and the solitude of its vantage point offers the opportunity for reflection:

> *Silent Nymph,* with curious Eye!
> Who, the purple Evening, lye
> On the mountain's lonely van,
> Beyond the Noise of busy man,
> Painting fair the form of Things,
> While the yellow Linnet sings;
> Or the tuneful Nightingale
> Charms the Forest with her Tale;
> Come with all thy various Hues,
> Come, and aid thy Sister Muse;
> Now while *Phœbus* riding high
> Gives Lustre to the Land and Sky!
> *Grongar Hill* invites my Song,
> Draw the Landskip bright and strong;
> *Grongar,* in whose Mossie Cells

Sweetly-musing Quiet dwells:
Grongar, in whose silent Shade,
For the modest Muses made,
So oft I have, the Even still.
At the Fountain of a Rill,
Sate upon a flow'ry Bed,
With my Hand beneath my Head;
And stray'd my Eyes o'er *Towy's* Flood,
Over Mead, and over Wood,
From House to House, from Hill to Hill,
'Till Contemplation had her fill.   (1-26)
History is invoked in the 'Old Castles' that 'on the Cliffs arise, / Proudly
tow'ring in the Skies' (51-52); and the busy concerns of society are rejected in
favour of the pleasures of rural solitude:

Be full, ye Courts, be great who will;
Search for Peace, with all your Skill:
Open wide the lofty Door,
Seek her on the marble Floor,
In vain ye search, she is not there;
In vain ye search the Domes of Care!
Grass and Flowers Quiet treads,
On the Meads, and Mountain-heads,
Along with Pleasure, close ally'd,
Ever by each other's Side:
And often, by the murm'ring Rill,
Hears the Thrush, while all is still,
Within the Groves of *Grongar HilL*   (148-60)

51   TYGER'S LETTER TO CAROLINE
With unmistakable sureness of touch James Austen locates the poem within
the boundaries of a child's world – kitchen, bedroom, farm – and peoples it
with the figures with whom she would be on terms of easy familiarity.
5   *Harriet* The cook.
10   *I slept a little on the dough* Thereby stopping it rising.
13   *barm* The froth formed on the top of fermenting malt liquor used for
       leavening bread.
39   *fat* I.e. her healthy plumpness.

52   ADDRESS TO TYGER
This poem gives an idea of the robust and unsentimental way in which
children were spoken to in the eighteenth and early nineteenth centuries. In
this, as in the previous one, Caroline's cat is charmingly characterised – her

father is at his most endearingly humorous; and yet the threat that if it misbehaves again it will be shot and hung up in a gamekeeper's larder, where apparently another cat of the same litter has already gone, makes a mockingly grim (though entirely plausible) conclusion.

10   *Micænas* A patron of the arts (from the adviser to Augustus and patron of Horace and Virgil).

13   *when you slept upon the dough* See 'Tyger's Letter to Caroline', above.

32   *guttling appetite* To guttle is 'to eat voraciously; to gormandize' (OED).

43   *Corbet* The farm bailiff at Steventon (see *Letters*, p.73).

50   *A lesson to the tabby race* Perhaps recalling Gray's celebrated *Ode on the Death of a Favourite Cat Drowned in a Tub of Gold Fishes*, a similarly unsentimental treatment of Selima, 'Demurest of the tabby kind', who, having stretched to reach the fish, 'tumbled headlong in'.

53   TO EDWARD ON PLANTING A LIME TREE ON THE TERRACE IN THE MEADOW BEFORE THE HOUSE

This poem is a meditation on time and memory, and is perhaps one of the most touching that James Austen wrote. He sees the lime tree that he and Edward plant together as a focus both for his memories of his son's childhood and, in years to come, for Edward's of his parents, by then long dead.

Steventon rectory was demolished, but the lime tree remains (see Deirdre Le Faye, 'The Lime Tree at Steventon Rectory', Jane Austen Society *Report* for 2000).

10   *a kind farewell* Edward entered Winchester College in 1814.

36   *Cowper's mother* In his poem *On the Receipt of my Mother's Picture* Cowper honours his mother, who died when he was a child, with an 'artless song' and recalls 'Thy nightly visits to my chamber made, / That thou mightst know me safe and warmly laid'.

70   *the little spireless Fane* In ch.2 of the *Memoir* James Edward Austen-Leigh quotes the phrase in his description of Steventon church, adding that he was speaking of it 'as it then was, before the improvements made by the present rector' (i.e. his cousin the Revd William Knight).

73   *your cousin's welcome guest* The living of Steventon was in the gift of Edward Knight, who intended it for his fourth son, William, when he was old enough; William succeeded Henry Austen (who held it for three years after James's death) in 1822 and retained it for fifty years.

82   *terrace* 'Along the upper or southern side of this garden, ran a terrace of the finest turf, which must have been in the writer's [i.e. Jane Austen's] thoughts when she described Catherine Morland's childish delight in "rolling down the green slope at the back of the house"' (*Memoir*, ch.2) Far from being able to 'retrace' 'each feature', James

Edward wrote to his sister, Anna Lefroy, after a visit in the late 1860s, 'All traces of former things are even more obliterated than I had expected. Even the terrace has been levelled, & its site is to be distinguished only by the finer turf on that place... One Lime planted by our father near that part has become a magnificent tree.' (HRO 23M93/84/1)

83   *fading* James describes the appearance of the wood both as it is then, in January, as they plant the tree, and generally in the hunting season.

87   *whilome* Once.

    your favourite steed Either the pony whose death was commemorated in an earlier poem (see above, p35) or Sutton, the one that succeeded it and was, according to Caroline, 'a most useful animal, carrying anybody on the road, and taking his young master with the hounds' (*Reminiscences*, p.25).

92   *The woodwalk* '...the chief beauty of Steventon consisted in its hedgerows. A hedgerow, in that country, does not mean a thin formal line of quickset, but an irregular border of copse-wood and timber, often wide enough to contain within it a winding footpath, or a rough cart track.... Two such hedgerows radiated, as it were, from the parsonage garden. One, a continuation of the turf terrace, proceeded westward, forming the southern boundary of the home-meadows; and was formed into a rustic shrubbery, with occasional seats, entitled "The Wood Walk".' (*Memoir*, ch.2)

97   *haply* Perhaps.

56   ULYSSES ANNOUNCES TO HECUBA THAT THE MANES OF ACHILLES DEMAND THE SACRIFICE OF POLYXENA

An MS poem with this title exists in the hand of James Edward Austen-Leigh (HRO 23M93/86/5/2) dating from the same period, when Edward was being prepared for entrance to Winchester; it is therefore possible that James set it for him and decided to write his own version. James was in the habit of discussing the classics with his son: in an undated letter written to him while he was at Oxford, James told him: 'I shall take your advice in not attempting the Trachinian Virgins – Sophocles and I have probably parted for ever. It is too late in the day, at 54, to be fagging at Greek Choruses. So I content myself with reading Thucydides again,– which is quite as much as my poor head is equal to. – I blunder also through a few pages of Tacitus most days. (HRO 23M93/MI Fiche 123) The source of the story in the present poem is the Epic Cycle and was treated by, among others, Euripides, Seneca, Ovid and Quintus of Smyrna. After the fall of Troy, Achilles, requiring sacrifice from beyond the grave, demands that Hecuba's daughter Polyxena should be killed.

    Manes Shades of the dead.

1   *"Grateful I hail the morn's returning light* Edward's poem opens more dramatically:

> Yes still the same, though Priams Towers fall
> Though royal slaughter stain the sacred wall,
> Though reft of Crown, of Country, Sons, & Lord,
> A wretched captive to a Foe abhorred,
> That Air of Majesty, that stately Mein,
> To all around her still proclaim the Queen,
> Unhappy Hecuba all these bereft,
> Yet hast thou still one darling comfort left,
> For fair as Helens self, & good as fair,
> One daughter sooths a captive Mother's Care,
> Still mayst thou weep with her oer former pain,
> And live a life of suffering oer again...

41   *his affianced bride* The story that Achilles, during his life, had loved Polyxena was a later accretion.

53   *Aulis* In *Iphigenia in Aulis* by Euripides Calchas predicts that the sacrifice of Iphigenia, daughter of Agamemnon and Clytemnestra, will be necessary to obtain a favourable wind for the Greek ships to leave the harbour.

77   *Calchas* The seer.

95   *Peleus son* Achilles was the son of Peleus and Thetis. The debate about his armour is the subject of the thirteenth book of Ovid's *Metamoiphoses*, which deals with the story of Hecuba and Polyxenes.

142   *what Christians since have known* James's attempt to wrench a Christian moral out of Greek myth is hardly a happy one. It is perhaps no coincidence that at the time he wrote this he was enthusiastically helping to set up a District Committee of the SPCK for Basingstoke and Alton.

143   *Niobe* The mythical queen of Thebes who, after the killing of all her children by Apollo and Artemis, asked Zeus to turn her to stone on Mount Sipylus.

60   MORNING – TO EDWARD

Writing while Edward was still at home being prepared for Winchester, James encourages him to work during the morning (i.e. in the period up to dinner time, probably about 4 o'clock), rather than follow only such pleasurable pursuits as hunting, fishing and shooting. The labourer sets an example, though of course for Edward work means study, specifically that of classical literature; and characteristically James looks forward to the time when 'The Nerves will flag, the spirits sink' and 'Rheumatism, Age or Gout' will prevent him leading an active life, and make him glad of a well stocked mind.

1   *once more the Sun* cf. Bishop T. Ken:

Awake, my soul, and with the sun
Thy daily stage of duty run
10   *Homestall* Farmyard.

36   *haply* Perhaps.

54   *parish bread* Until the Poor Law Amendment Act of 1834, even the able-bodied poor were able to obtain some relief from the poor rate without entering a workhouse.

63   *time mispent* cf. 'Awake, my soul':
Redeem thy mis-spent time that's past;
Live this day as if 'twere thy last..

70   *novels* The implication that novels do not provide improvement for the mind would not have pleased Jane Austen, who both in her letters and, famously, in *Northanger Abbey* strongly defended the form (see pp.37-38).

94   *cassino* Casino was one of the fashionable card games; Lady Middleton plays it at the party in London when Marianne encounters Willoughby (see *Sense and Sensibility*, p.175).

101   *King of Pyle* Nestor, king of Pylos, the oldest and wisest of the Greek generals, who was in the habit of giving lengthy advice.

102   *the Lord of Ithac's Isle* Odysseus.

103   *Calypso's charms* In Bk I of *The Odyssey* Calypso offers Odysseus immortality if he will stay with her, but he resists.

104   *Circe's cup* With which she turned men into swine.

110   *The pious Chieftain's labour long* The twelve books of *The Æneid* trace Æneas's acts from his escape from Troy to his settlement in Italy.

149   *the wild horrors of the storm* See Thomson,*The Seasons*, 'Summer', 1103-71.

151   *Old Ocean's near approaching swell* cf. *The Seasons:*
The stars obtuse emit a shiver'd ray;
Or frequent seem to shoot athwart the gloom,
And long behind them trail the whitening blaze.
Snatch'd in short eddies, plays the withered leaf;
And on the flood the dancing feather floats. ('Winter', 127-32)

Assiduous, in his bower, the wailing owl
Plies his sad song. The cormorant on high
Wheels from the deep, and screams along the land.
Loud shrieks the soaring hern; and with wild wing
The circling sea-fowl cleave the flaky clouds.
Ocean, unequal press'd, with broken tide
And blind commotion heaves... (Ibid., 144-50)

167   *Southey's wild fantastic muse* Southey was the nephew of the Revd

Herbert Hill, who married Jane's friend Catherine Bigg. In 1808 Jane wrote to Cassandra of his *Letters from England; by Dom Manuel Alvarez Espriella:* 'The Man describes well, but is horribly anti-english. He deserves to be the foreigner he assumes.' (*Letters*, 141)

171 *Cœlebs* The Evangelical Hannah More's *Cœlebs in Search of a Wife* was published in 1809 and Cassandra tried to persuade Jane to read it. 'You have by no means raised my curiosity after Caleb; – My disinclination for it before was affected, but now it is real; I do not like the Evangelicals. – Of course I shall be delighted when I read it, like other people, but till I do, I dislike it.' (*Letters*, pp.169-70) Whether or not she did ever read it is not known; the only other reference to it in her letters is to remonstrate about Cassandra's pointing out that she had got the name wrong: 'I am not at all ashamed about the name of the Novel, having been guilty of no insult towards your handwriting; the Diphthong I always saw, but knowing how fond you were of adding a vowel wherever you could, I attributed it to that alone – & the knowledge of the truth does the book no service;—the only merit it could have, was in the name of Caleb, which has an honest, unpretending sound; but in Cœlebs, there is pedantry & affectation. – Is it written only to Classical Scholars?' (*Letters*, p.172) In fact, she may have confused the name with that of William Godwin's Caleb Williams (1794).

172 *ragouts* Stews.

65 EVENING – TO EDWARD

This continues the theme of the benefits of labour and the undesirability of indolence; but it is now seen from the perspective of evening, both literally, when the peasant, returning home, finds the rewards of his day's work, and metaphorically when in the evening of our life we shall find our efforts rewarded in heaven.

24 *cot* Cottage.

67 ON REFUSING A SPECIAL INVITATION FROM M^R. CHUTE TO MEET HIS HOUNDS AT M^R. VILLEBOIS COVER, CHILTON WOOD

James Edward Austen-Leigh gives an account of the occasion in *Recollections of the Early Days of the Vine Hunt:* 'It happened that on May 6, 1814, after regular hunting had ceased, by some arrangement between the two masters, Mr. Chute's hounds were to have a private meet at Mr. Vilebois' cover, Chilton Wood [by Candover]. My father was invited to it. He was then preparing me at home for Winchester School, and, to my great disappointment, declined the invitation; but in order to console me wrote the following lines, which though destitute of the poetry which is to be found in some of his compositions, yet contains plenty of good sense.' (p.27) William Chute kept his own foxhounds at The Vyne, near Basingstoke; Truman Villebois was master of the neighbouring Hampshire Hunt.

8   *"For all on earth there is a season'*, 'To every thing there is a season' *(Ecclesiastes* III.i).

9   *an ancient Prince Ecclesiastes* was formerly attributed to Solomon.

29   *sainfoin* Plant grown for forage.

44   *members great* William Chute was MP for Hampshire.
      brewers rich The Curtis family, who kept the Angel Inn in Basingstoke, hunted regularly.

48   *George* George Hickson, Mr Chute's huntsman.

54   *Doctor Henry Gabell* Headmaster of Winchester College, 1810-23.

55   *Wykeham's rule* Winchester College was founded in 1378 by William of Wykeham, Bishop of Winchester.

70   LINES WRITTEN AT STEVENTON

In this poem we have for the first time the impression that James Austen has become an invalid. He is already conscious of his age (though in fact he was not yet fifty) and aware of the fact that he is not always an easy man to live with. Steventon rectory had been his childhood home and he had occupied it as curate and subsequently rector since 1801, so it is not surprising that even the prospect of a larger stipend should fail to tempt him away from it now. During the course of the poem, James undertakes an objective view of his family life; and after a description of the rather dull, featureless North Oxfordshire plain, makes a smooth transition to the familiar country surrounding his beloved village.

6   the *Patriarch* Abraham (see *Genesis* XII.i).

14   *pitch my tent* 'And he removed from thence unto a mountain on the east of Bethel, and pitched his tent, having Bethel on the west, and Hai on the east: and there he builded an altar unto the Lord.' *(Genesis* XII.viii)

105   *A numerous party* An echo here, perhaps, of the outing to Sotherton (see *Mansfield Park*, Vol.II.pp.80-83)? The novel had appeared a few months before the poem was written.

120   *Authors too ourselves* All three of James's children wrote, and like the rest of the Austen family delighted in verses, riddles and charades. Subsequently they were each to write their account of the family and Aunt Jane, though only James Edward's *Memoir* was intended for publication.

125   *cat or pony* See *Tyger's Letter to Caroline, Address to Tyger* and *To Edward on the death of his first pony.*

168   *nature's sketches* James Austen characteristically employs the language of the artist.

177   *haulm* Stalks.

185   *plenteous dearth* An effective oxymoron.

195   *Charwell* The River Cherwell joins the Thames (or Isis) at Oxford.

211   *our small domain* 'The house itself stood in a shallow valley, surrounded by sloping meadows, well sprinkled with elm trees, at the end of a small village of cottages, each well provided with a garden, scattered about prettily on either side of the road.' (James Edward Austen-Leigh, *A Memoir of Jane Austen*, ch.2)

229   *nice* In this context, over particular.

230   *homestall* Farmyard.

        our tasteless sires The rectory was pulled down for the Revd William Knight in 1824 and replaced with a new building on the other side of the valley.

240   *Manor house* ... a fine old manor-house, of Henry VIII's time, occupied by a family named Digweed, who have for more than a century rented it, together with the chief farm in the parish' *(Memoir*, ch.2). After many alterations, the manor house was demolished in the 20th century.

251   *Raleigh's valued root* An unnecessary periphrasis in an otherwise simple and unpretentious poem.

277   *haply* Perhaps.

77   AUTUMN

From the cheerful repudiation of spring at the beginning of the poem as a season fit for 'younger, gayer poets' to sing, and the acceptance of autumn as the appropriate time of year for those 'of ripe and graver age', James Austen progresses to a consideration of the bleak classical view of man's whole life as 'one autumnal day'. This in turn leads him to a Christian affirmation of the Resurrection and thence to a neat return to spring, now triumphantly reasserted as a symbol of eternal life. The structure of the poem is deftly handled and the reversal of the beginning at the end comes as a pleasurable surprise.

27   *joy and woe* See n. above, p.163.

102   *homestall* Farmyard.

112   *mind and heart* cf. *Evening – to Edward*, 52.

134   "*pale declining year*" The phrase, not in Thomson, comes from Baron van Swieten's libretto for Haydn's oratorio (1801), translated by van Swieten himself, at the begirming of 'Winter' (No.29, 'Now sinks the pale declining year'). Clementi brought out a vocal score in England in 1813.

139   "*sear and yellow leaf*"   '...my way of life

        Is fall'n into the sere, the yellow leaf...'   (*Macbeth*, V.iii. 22-23)

161   *the Roman bard* Virgil. In Book VI of *The Æneid*, the Sybil conducts Æneas to the underworld.

174 *the fabled King of Crete* Minos, who at his death became a judge in the underworld.

83 THE AUTUMN WALK — TO MARY
The title recalls V and VI of Cowper's *The Task* – respectively 'The Winter Morning Walk' and 'The Winter Walk at Noon'. Urging Mary to give up her work until the evening, James describes the simple pleasures of a walk through the autumnal woods and fields round Steventon, and, on returning, the cosiness of their candlelit room. The contemplation of approaching winter is counterpointed by the anticipation of Edward's return from Winchester for the Christmas holidays.

18   *vest* Loose gown (Caroline was ten at the time the poem was written).
55   *Elm encircled* A favourite term of James Austen's: see *To Edward – On planting a lime tree on the terrace*, 1.86.
57   *leasing* Gleaning. A contrast is made between the poor, who labour to gather up wheat and nuts, and the farmer, who complacently watches his 'numerous flock' pass by. Both, however, are part of a balanced rural economy enjoying the 'plenty' distributed by a generous Providence and therefore equally 'please the sight'.
79   *coze* Chat familiarly.
96   *Cressy* The Battle of Crécy (1346), where the Black Prince won his spurs. *Waterloo* Where Napoleon lost his.
99   *the pale declining year* See n. to *Autumn*, above, p.178.
115   *my Sunday's ride* To Sherborne St John, a living he held in plurality with Steventon and other parishes.
119   *Venta's towers* The cathedral in Winchester has only one tower, but there are others among the various churches and chapels in the city. Venta Belgarum was the Roman name for Winchester.
         Itchen's stream The River Itchen runs through Winchester.
120   *youthful bard* William Lisle Bowles wrote his sonnet 'To the River Itchin' at the age of 25; but it is possible that James Austen is also thinking of some early poem of his own about Winchester that has not come to light.

86   'VENTA! WITHIN THY SACRED FANE'
James Austen's tribute to his sister was written shortly after her death and is her poetic memorial; the 'bitter tear' dropped on her bier by her grieving brothers conveys, as an image, a distinct impression of funeral marble. There is a clearly defined structure: the opening address to the restmg-place of the mighty provides a grandiose setting, architecturally and, in terms of the elegy, verbally, for the 'fair form and fairer mind' of the sister who is interred in both cathedral and poem; then, after a tribute to the literary and domestic

179

labours that, creditably, she found not to be incompatible, the final section of the poem speculates on the nature of the human state after death, as, in the convention of the elegy, her spirit is sent on its heavenward journey.

1   *Venta* Venta Belgarum was the Roman name for Winchester.
      fane Temple.
      There are several possible influences on the opening lines of the poem:

> See yonder Hallow'd Fane! the pious Work
> Of Names once fam'd, now dubious or forgot,
> And buried 'midst the Wreck of Things which were:
> There lie interr'd the more illustrious Dead.
>
>   (Robert Blair, *The Grave*)
>
> Where Venta's Norman castle still uprears
> Its rafter'd hall, that o'er the grassy foss,
> And scatter'd flinty fragments clad in moss,
> On yonder steep in naked state appears...
>
>   (Thomas Warton, *On King Arthur's Round Table*
>   *at Winchester*)

2   *many a chief* The remains of Saxon kings originally buried in the Old Minster, which stood adjacent to the present cathedral, were transferred to mortuary chests placed over the presbytery screens in 1525.

6   *Gothic choir* The construction of the great retrochoir at the beginning of the 13th century more than doubled the area of the original east end.
      Pillared Aisle I.e. the nave, with its soaring Perpendicular pillars.

10   *Coffins* The mortuary chests referred to above.

12   *the Conquerors haughty Son* A 12th-century tomb in the choir is supposedly that of William Rufus.

15   *honoured Wickham* William of Wykeham (c.1323-1404), Chancellor of England and founder of New College, Oxford and Winchester College, as Bishop of Winchester remodelled the original Norman nave of the cathedral.

18   *Old Walkelyn's heavier style* The Norman bishop Walkelin was responsible for the Romanesque building.

38   *'Which dying, she would wish to blot'* cf. Ben Jonson's remark (in *Discoveries, De Shakespeare Nostrat*) of Shakespeare: in his writing (whatsoever he penned) he never blotted out a line.'

71-2 *By Seraphs born... While Angles gladden at the sight* A conventional enough image (if a somewhat unconventional spelling, particularly for a clergyman), it gains a special appropriateness here by the presence at the other end of the North Aisle of the 'Guardian Angels' Chapel' with its 13th-century vault paintings of angels.

Caroline Austen wrote: 'In September [1817] my father had a serious attack of illness, and from that period I date his rapid decline. He never recovered to even the very poor state of health which had been his portion through many previous years, for as long as my memory could go back. But he did get better, and in October went to Worthing for change of air.' *(Reminsicences,* p.50) This is the last major completed poem of James Austen and is one of his most ambitious. The autumnal scene combines with the effects of recent illness to turn his thoughts towards mortality and the importance of having lived a useful life. Yet the vision is anything but morbid: 'The world / Is full of wonders', as a generous Providence ensures that 'every year displays / The miracle of harvest'; and as, in a final scene of quiet evening domesticity amid the family circle that meant so much to him, he reads aloud the lines that he has been writing, the poem concludes with its own achievement.

12 *Its size augmenting while it moves along* This is beautifully observed, as indeed is the whole harvest scene, which is composed as if it were a painting.

21 *leasers* Gleaners. cf. Thomson's *The Seasons:*

> The gleaners spread around, and here and there,
> Spike after spike, their scanty harvest pick. ('Autumn', 167-68)

98 *haply* Perhaps.

130 *"with our hearts / To commune in our chambers, & be still"* Psalm IV v.4: 'Stand in awe, and sin not: commune with your own heart, and in your chamber, and be still.'

145 *the sun's meridian disk / Emerging, dissipates the vapoury cloud* There is possibly an echo of Cowper here:

> 'Tis morning; and the sun, with ruddy orb
> Ascending, fires the horizon; while the clouds,
> That crowd away before the driving wind,
> More ardent as the disk emerges more,
> Resemble most some city in a blaze,
> Seen through the leafless wood.
> ('The Winter Morning Walk', 1-6)

173 *our talent* This refers to the parable of the talents, *Matt.* XXV.xiv-xxx. Its best known poetic use is Milton's 'that one talent which is death to hide / Lodged with me useless' (*On His Blindness*, 3-4).

181 *the Circean cup* See line 104 above, p.175. James Austen may be thinking of Milton's *Comus:*

> Who knows not Circe,
> The daughter of the Sun? whose charmed cup
> Whoever tasted, lost his upright shape,

And downward fell into a groveling swine. (50-53)

186   *wildered* Bewildered.

204   *time misspent* See line 63 above, p175.

221   *"whet/My almost blunted purpose"* Hamlet III.iv: 'this visitation / Is but to whet thy almost blunted purpose' (110-11)

257   *besprent* Scattered

277   *Glover's hand* John Glover (1767-1849) was a landscape watercolourist and in 1813 was president of the Society of Painters in Water-Colours. Jane Austen referred to him in a letter of 1812 (see *Letters*, p.195).

300   *Lord of all I see around* cf. Cowper, *Verses Supposed to be written by Alexander Selkirk, during his solitary abode in the island of Juan Fernandez*:

> I am monarch of all I survey,
> My right there is none to dispute;
> From the centre all round to the sea
> I am lord of the fowl and the brute. (1-4)

326   *The manor house, converted to a farm* In Sherborne St John the moated Manor Farm was believed locally to have been a manor house in earlier times, and was so described on a map of 1732.

353   *nice* Precise.

364   *manna* See Exodus XVI.xv.

365   *quails* See Exodus XVI.xiii.

431   *all cold & cheerless* An unconscious echo, perhaps, of Gloucester in *King Lear*: 'All dark and comfortless' (III.vii. 84)?

445   *Th'Historian's record* In Bk IV of *The Task* ('The Winter Evening'), Cowper also describes the pleasures of reading and conversation among the family circle:

> The poet's or historian's page by one
> Made vocal for the amusement of the rest... (158-59)
>
> Discourse ensues, not trivial, yet not dull... (174)

454   *by partial kindness led* cf.*Lines written at Steventon*, 120-22, above, p.73.

99   THE ŒCONOMY OF RURAL LIFE

The longest and most ambitious of James Austen's poems, which he spent the last months of his life writing and which was unfinished when he died, is a discussion of the values and obligations of life in the country. Moral hints can be drawn from nature: though some value rural life for its sports and pastimes, intellectual lessons are to be had from studies of astronomy, botany or geography; and since the mind must have 'resources in itself', reading is important. But the land also offers opportunities for the exercise of charity in visits, gifts or the creation of employment for the poor; such actions are not only good in themselves but they also make the person who does them aware of the blessings of his own existence. Kindness, however, should be bestowed only on the deserving poor; and from them genuine gratitude will be obtained, an example of which James cites in the narrative of his own farm balliff. But there must be care of the souls as well as of the bodies of the poor: and in a strongly worded passage that proved to be the last part of the poem to be written, the Bible and especially the Prayer Book are invoked as essential tools in saving the poor from the dangers of Calvinism and the influence o Dissenting preachers.

10   *"And little of this great world... " Othello,* I.iii:
> And little of this great world can I speak,
> More than pertains to feats of broil and battle... (86-7)

18   *"Tongues in the trees..." As You Like It,* II.i:
> And this our life, exempt from public haunt,
> Finds tongues in trees, books in the running brooks,
> Sermons in stones, and good in everything. (15-17)

44   *By Gilpin or by Price* William Gilpin, the authority on the picturesque, was an early favourite of Jane Austen, according to her brother Henry's 'Biographical Notice' (*Northanger Abbey,* p.7); he and James no doubt encouraged her to read him. The *Essay on the Picturesque* by Sir Uvedale Price (1794) was a much read and very influential work on the subject.

56   *some Villa small* James Austen's gentle mockery of the urban aspiration to rural gentility is aptly expressed through the appropriation of elements of fashionable garden design (chinoiserie, Strawberry Hill Gothic, the Italianate poplar) for the decoration of neat palings surrounding a house 'hard by the dusty road'. The tiny carriage sweep, the restricted hedge and the small garden all add to the image of an estate in miniature proportions.

61   *two perches & a half* About 75 square yards.

97   *cerulean* Deep blue.

98   *elastic* Buoyant.

108   *what time* A poetic archaism found in Milton and elsewhere.

122   *beans expanding leaf* James Austen is referring to the horse bean, grown for cattle fodder or to be ground into beanmeal for coarse bread.

130   *Rout* A large evening party.

136   *Club* Gentlemen in the country met on regular evenings in dining clubs, as General Tilney does (*Northanger Abbey,* p.210); there were also whist clubs such as the one held at the Crown in Highbury (see *Emma,* p.197). cf. *Epilogue to the Sultan,* 22-39, p.28.

140   *gape seed* Something to be stared at.

157   *haply* By chance.

167   *Euclid* Greek mathematician whose texts on geometry were the basis of teaching the subject in schools.

the Stagyrite The Greek philosopher Aristotle was born in Stagira.

184   *Circean cup* See above, p.92.

192   *German Scoliast* Commentaries, or scholia, on classical texts were assiduously produced in German during the 18th century.

196   *records old* James Austen had always placed a high value on reading history. Thirty years earlier he had written in *The Loiterer*: '... historic knowledge will justly claim the highest rank amongst our literary acquirements. ...the use as well as pleasure of historic studies extend themselves over every land, where the muses have fixed their residence; and are the constant attendants of genius, taste, and learning.' (No.7)

199   *The well enlightened Spirit of our Sires* James was remarkably consistent in this opinion. In the same essay in *The Loiterer* he had written: 'The muse of history... never appears in a more engaging attitude, than when recommending the actions of their ancestors to the notice of British youth.—The deeds of the brave and the hardy are the best study for the noble and the free, and we are under too many obligations to our ancestors, for the happy effects of their virtues, not to take an early opportunity of knowing more intimately, and admiring more warmly, the excellence of our Constitution, and the wisdom of its Founders.'

215   *Clarendon or Hume* The Earl of Clarendon's *History of the Rebellion* (1702-4) gave an eyewitness account of the English Civil Wars. *The History of England* (1759-62) was the most popular work of the Scottish philosopher and historian David Hume; Jane Austen owned a copy, and in *Northanger Abbey* Eleanor Tilney reads it 'with pleasure' (p.109).

219   *Liberty* One of the themes of Hume's *History of England* is the development of liberty and the conditions that make it possible.

222   *mimic Patriots* The term 'patriot' had become increasingly suspect: 'mimic' here implies a false claim to the values of the real patriot. cf Cowper:

> To see a band call'd patriot for no cause,
> But that they catch at popular applause   *(Table Talk*, 143-44)

263   *Judah's king* Solomon, who 'spake of trees, from the cedar tree that is in Lebanon even unto the hyssop that springeth out of the wall' (*I Kings* IV.xxxiii).

292   *Donald* Donald Bean Lean, In Sir Walter Scott's *Waverley* (1814).

294   *Waverley's enthusiastic mind* Edward Waverley, the hero of Scott's novel, is led by his romantic temperament to join the Jacobites. *Waverley* was an outstanding success and determined Scott to turn from poetry to a career as a novelist. In a letter of September 1814 Jane Austen wrote: 'Walter Scott has no business to write novels, especially good ones.– It is not fair.– He has Fame & Profit enough as a Poet, and should not be taking the bread out of other people's mouths. – I do not like him, & do

not mean to like Waverley if I can help it—but fear I must.' *(Letters,* p.277)

298   *Elspeth* Elspeth Mucklebackit, the old grandmother in the fisher's hut in Scott's *The Antiquary* (1816).

301   *Jeanie Deans* In Scott's *The Heart of Midlothian* (1818) she walks to London to secure a pardon from Queen Caroline for her sister, Effie, who has been convicted of child murder.

334   *"'Tis charity, my reader, charity"* Unidentified.

351   *The "icy fang of winter" As You Like It,* II.i:
> the icy fang
> And churlish chiding of the winter's wind (6-7)

374   *Vestry* The church vestry was responsible for administering the Poor Law in the parish.

381   *the skilful Leech* Physician. By the beginning of the 19th century the term was used largely as a jocular term and it may here be intended as a proper name.

399   twice *bless'd* From Portia's speech in *The Merchant of Venice:*
> The quality of mercy is not strain'd,
> It droppeth as the gentle rain from heaven
> Upon the place beneath: it is twice bless'd;
> It blesseth him that gives and him that takes... (IV.i. 184-7)

425   *One half the world* A gentle rebuke, perhaps, to Emma's observation that 'One half of the world cannot understand the pleasures of the other' *(Emma,* p.81)? Jane Austen herself noted that James and his wife did not like *Emma* 'so well as either of the 3 others'; *(Minor Works,* p.436).

459   *the farinaceous root / By Raleigh first imported* In the context of a serious discussion of poverty such a laboured circumlocution sounds faintly absurd.

461   *Guyana's mines* In 1595 Raleigh led an expedition up the Orinoco which he described in *A Discovery of the Empire of Guyana.*

536   *One such I daily see* John Bond, the farm bailiff at Steventon. For details of his life see D. Dean Cantrell, 'John Bond: A Source for William Larkins?', *Collected Reports of the Jane Austen Society* Vol.3, pp.339-44 and Deirdre Le Faye, 'James Austen's poetical biography of John Bond', *Collected Reports* Vol.4, pp.243-47.

573   *To Bath* Mr Austen moved with his wife and daughters to Bath in1801.

575   *a kind neighbour* James Holder, of Ashe Park.

586   *One morn* The fire took place on 6 March 1808, as the Revd J.H.G. Lefroy, rector of Ashe, wrote to his brother Edward on 9 March 1808: 'Last Sunday morning early a fire broke out in two Tenements at Steventon belonging to M[r] Edw[d] Austen in about [3]/[4] of an hour reduced them to a bare shell & entirely burnt down a barn adjoining in which was lodged

about £80 worth of Corn belonging to the Digweeds which of course was consumed. The Bonds who lived in one of the Tenements with difficulty saved themselves & a little furniture but a poor old man & woman who inhabited the other end were so dreadfully burnt that the Woman has since died and the man's life is scarcely expected.' It will be noted that James's account does not entirely square with Mr Lefroy's.

621   *like Orlando* See *As You Like It*, II.vi.

637   *"Frosty, but kindly"* In offering to go with Orlando as his servant, Adam declares:

> my age is as a lusty winter
> Frosty, but kindly.   (*As You Like It*, II.iv. 52-3)

645   *haply* By chance.

679   *the poor man's best/And safest comment on the Scripture text* On 19 August 1813, James Austen delivered a speech to the first meeting of the SPCK Branch at Basingstoke in which he expressed the same view of the Prayer Book: '...the Society for promoting Christian Knowledge... has always distributed, not the Bible only, but a variety of Religious Tracts explanatory of its Doctrines and Duties – and that best of all Commentaries, to a Member of our Establishment, the Liturgy of the Church of England. It not only puts the Bible into a poor man's hand, but provides him with the best means of understanding it.' (MS in the hand of Anna Lefroy in the Chawton album of James Austen's verses. See Irene Collins, 'Too much zeal for the Bible Society: Jane Austen, her family, and the Religious Quarrels of her time', Jane Austen Society *Report* for 2001, where the speech is printed in full.

694   *Antinomian error* The view that Christians are released from the obligation to observe any moral law.

696   *assurance* The doctrine held by some Dissenters that salvation is assured.

697   *childhood's premature / Devout experience* Natural feeling, as opposed to a response to external authority.

701   *the bells "have knolled to Church,"* As You Like It, II.vii. 114.

709   *by the window, not the door* Though here the phrase is presumably intended metaphorically, Methodists and other preachers frowned on by the Church of England often had *to* make a surreptitious entrance (and even more often a hasty exit).

712   *"the Gospel fully preach'd"* '... from Jerusalem, and round about unto Illyricum, I have fully preached the gospel of Christ.' (*Romans* XIV. xix)

117   PSALMS VERSIFIED ABOUT THREE WEEKS BEFORE THE AUTHOR'S DEATH

James Austen was in a long tradition of psalm versifiers, among them some of the greatest poets in English, including Sir Philip Sidney, Milton, Herbert,

Crashaw and Vaughan. The most popular metrical version of the Psalter was that by Tate and Brady (1696), which was sung well into the 19th century, and which, in providing texts for singable tunes, had a practical purpose. To transform the magnificent language of the Authorized Version into stilted rhyming couplets seems a pointless and dispiriting activity, as a comparison of the opening of James's rendering of Psalm 137 with that in the Prayer Book ('By the waters of Babylon we sat down and wept: when we remembered thee, O Sion') will quickly show.

120 'A PLAIN THERE IS'
[Solution: Billiard Table]
26 *out of pocket* A splendid pun to end the verse.

120 'FOR HONESTY, TO SAY THE TRUTH'
[Solution: Miller]
15 *toll* Charge a toll; the word was often used of the charges levied by millers.

121 'IN A TIGHT LITTLE COTTAGE'
[Solution: Weather House]
9 *nice* Requiring a fine judgment.
12 *another adviser* Robert Boyle first exhibited his barometer in 1665; during the next century it became increasingly popular as a household object.

122 'SINGLY, TO POSSESS MY CHARMS'
[Solution: Garters]
6 *bless their stars* The single charm to which so many aspire refers of course to the Order of the Garter, which, as with all the orders of chivalry, has a star as part of its insignia.
12 *one lady* The Countess of Salisbury, who according to legend slipped her garter at a ball; it was gallantly picked up by Edward III, who thereby instituted the Order.

122 'SURE NEVER WAS CREATURE SO GROSSLY ABUSED'
[Solution: Post]
8 *I love to direct* I.e. a sign post.

123 'IF OUR COMPANY MAKES OUR TRUE CHARACTER KNOWN'
[Solution: Fiddle]
8 *a snug little friend* I.e. the bow.
13 *butter 'd pease* A country dance tune.
14 *roast beef* The song *Roast Beef of Old England* (1735).

16   *drops of brandy* A dance tune sometimes also known as 'Strip the Willow.

123   'OF STRANGE & COMPOUND FORM AM I'
      [Solution: Cedar pencil]

6   *always used me well* The reference is probably to Gilpin, whose travel books (among them one on the Lake District) were beautifully illustrated by the author.

7   *sceptic Whigs* Queen Anne was the last English monarch to touch for the King's Evil, or scrofula. Before her, William III had dismissed it as Popish superstition; and her successor, George I, who favoured the Whigs rather than the Church Party, never undertook it. Whilst it was considered to pertain to the Divine Right – something the Whigs abhorred – Anne herself repudiated the idea, seeing it rather as evidence of her right to the succession.

124   PEG NICHOLSONS & SHERIFF KNIGHTS STAND BY
      [Solution: Sir loin]

1   *Peg Nicholsons* Possibly from Burns's *Elegy on Willie Nichol's Mare* (1790):

>   Peg Nicholson was a good bay mare,
>   As ever trod on airn;
>   But now she's floating down the Nith,
>   And past the mouth o' Cairn.

It is difficult to see the connection; possibly a reference to a family joke. *Sheriff Knights* Edward Austen was High Sheriff of Kent in 1801, though he did not officially take the name of Knight until 1812.

124   'DIVIDED, OF AN ANCIENT HOUSE AM I'
      [Solution: A-loft]

125   'BY ALL PRUDENT FOLKS'
      [Solution: Housewife]

4   *in sight* The HRO reading makes little sense; it is almost certainly a miscopying of the Ch 'no right'.

125   'IN MY FIRST, THAT HE MAY NOT BE TARDY OR LATE'
      [Solution: Canterbury]

3   *Curate* I.e. a clergyman (cf. *Book of Common Prayer*: 'Send down upon our Bishops and Curates, and all Congregations committed to their charge, the healthful Spirit of thy grace...').

125   'IF THERE BE TRUTH IN PROVERBS OLD'
      [Solution: Waterloo]

4   *Knaves exult O'er Kings In* the round game of loo, Jack of Spades (known as 'Pam') is the highest card.

125   'MY FIRST A HORSEMAN'S DIRE DISGRACE WOULD TELL'
[Solution: Falstaff]
2   *longer by an L* A pun on 'ell'.
5   *Wight* Person.

126   MY FIRST CAN WELL FINISH A BOTTLE OF WINE'
[Solution: Eton]
1   *My first* I.e. the letter E.
3   *My second's large belly* A ton, or tun, was a wine cask.
6   *Castalia's rill* Castalia was a fountain of Parnassus sacred to the Muses; those who drank from it were inspired with the gift of poetry. This is a particularly neat and ingenious charade, since each of its elements is based on the same theme (drinking).

126   MY 2^d MAY IN YOUTH BE VERY CHARMING'
[Solution: Bridesmaid]

INDEX OF FIRST LINES

A plain there is, by wood surrounded	120
Amid the temperate hours of evening grave	3
As fair Eliza t'other day	11
Autumn's tints are on the trees	83
Beneath yon oak-crowned hill whose solemn shades	5
By all prudent folks, he a rash man is reckoned	125
Divided, of an ancient house am I	124
Ever honoured Mistress mine	51
For honesty, to say the truth	120
Gay Summer's sunny noons & evenings mild	88
"Grateful I hail the morn's returning light	56
Halloo! Good Gentlefolks! What none asleep!	9
I write to please my Caroline	37
If our company makes our true character known	123
If there be truth in proverbs old, my first	125
In a tight little cottage, whose straw cover'd roof	121
In barbarous times, e'er learning's sacred light	20
In every clime where science spreads her reign	23
In my first, that he may not be tardy or late	125
In this gay season, when midst genial showers	41
In those sad times, which once Britannia knew	21
Inconstant Month; whose varying face	33
Let Spring his green & rosy wreath display	18
Let younger, gayer Poets sing	77
Lord help us! What strange foolish things are these men	27
My First a Horseman's dire disgrace would tell	125
My first can well finish a bottle of Wine	126
My 2d may in youth be very charming	126
Night's shades are flown – once more the Sun	60
Nymph of the straw-crowned hat, & kirtle pale	15
Of rural life the enjoyments & the cares	99
Of strange & compound form am I	123
On a wild Moor, all brown and bleak	29
On such Subjects no Wonder that she shou'd write well	39
Once more my friends, by youthful fancy led	10
Parent of winning smiles & soft desires	15
Peg Nicholsons & Sheriff Knights stand by	124
Saved from proud Egypt's plagues, & Egypt's toil	119
Singly, to possess my charms	122
Spring Wood! thy verdant walks well pleased I view	14

Stern Monarch of the howling tempests hail!	14
Sure never was creature so grossly abused	122
Sure you are Tyger rightly named	52
Sweet maid, whose opening charms as morning fair	17
The sun is now set, & the deep glowing west	65
This morning was our wedding day	39
This tree which we together plant	53
Though I've hardly recovered myself from the fright	11
Through Berkshire's lanes & hedgerows green	44
Veiled in thy radiant vest of streaming light	16
Venta! within thy sacred fane	86
Well sings the Bard of Britain's happier age	26
What fondly cherish'd thoughts my bosom fill	16
When Sion's tribes, at Heaven's command	118
When Thespis first professed the mimic art	8
Where Babel's stream its world of waters pours	117
While you my Friend, with titles crowned	1
Why beats my heart with fear oppre'st	17
"Why must this morn be spent in books,"?	67
"Why weeps my boy?" his Father said	35
"Would you view Selbourne Hanger aright"	46
Ye fields & trees, amongst whose flowers & shade	70